FOLK

/ FŌK /

*noun: used as a friendly form
of address to a group of people*

*adjective: of or relating
to the traditional art or culture
of a community*

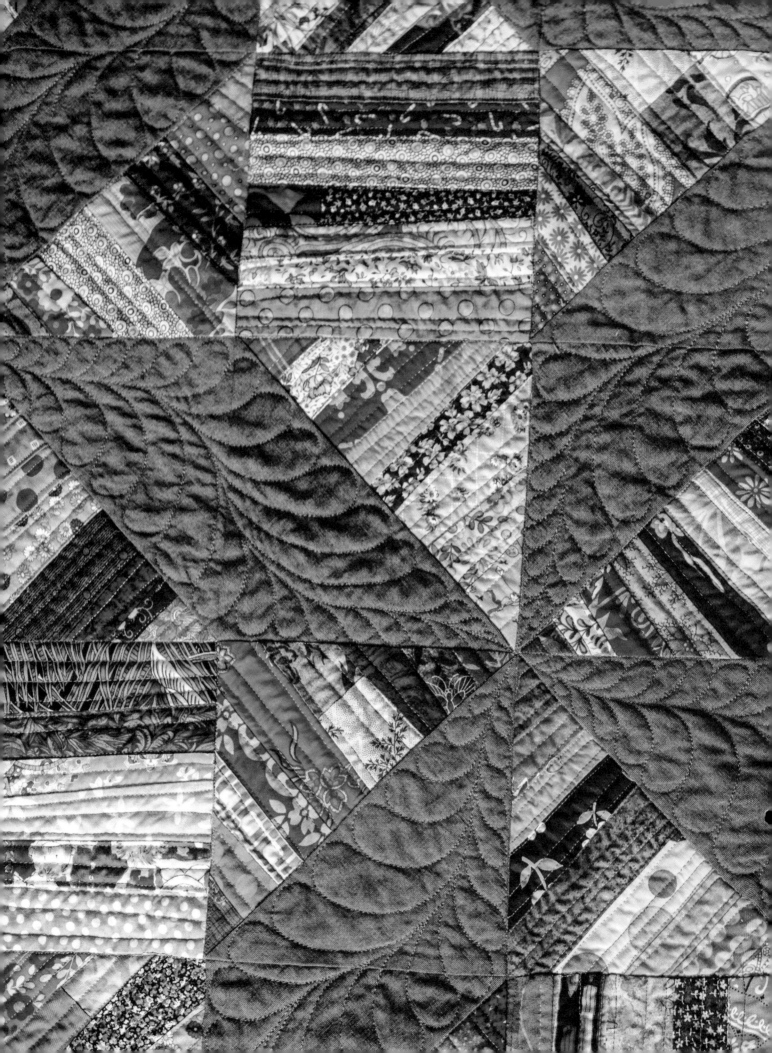

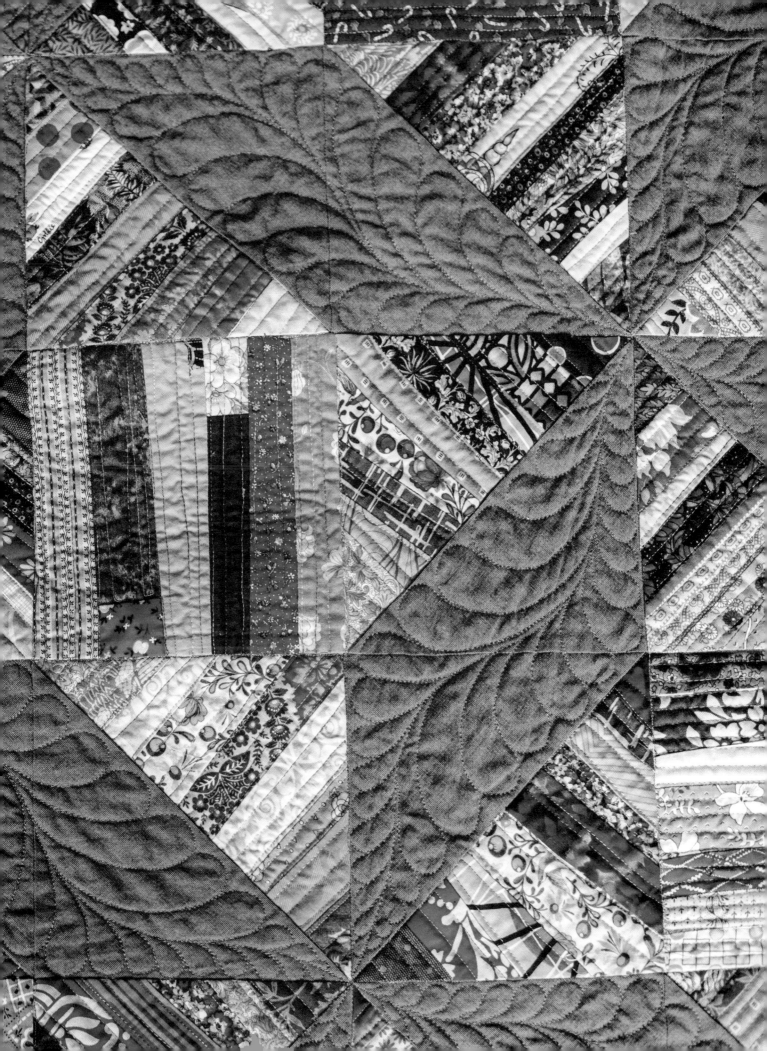

Quiltfolk

PUBLISHER *Michael McCormick*

EDITOR IN CHIEF *Mary Fons*

CREATIVE DIRECTOR *Janelle Frazier*

COPY EDITOR *Jenny Bartoy*

LEAD CONTENT DEVELOPER *Laura McDowell Hopper*

PHOTOGRAPHER *Melanie Zacek*

CONTRIBUTING WRITERS
Jennifer Ackerman-Haywood
Meg Cox

GUEST CONTRIBUTORS
American Quilt Study Group   *Marsha MacDowell*
Karen Lieberman   *Mary Worrall*

Quiltfolk is a community-supported quarterly.
Visit Quiltfolk.com.

SUBMISSIONS
submit@quiltfolk.com

QUESTIONS
hello@quiltfolk.com

 /quiltfolk   *@quiltfolk*   *@quiltfolk*

PO Box 10796, Eugene, OR 97440
Quiltfolk.com

OPPOSITE: A blue-and-white quilt (1960) by famed Michigan quilter Mary Schafer.
PREVIOUS PAGE: Detail, string-pieced scrap quilt by Lynn Carson Harris. "The small square patch of red print with a yellow apple was left over from a blouse I made in 1975," said Carson Harris. "I left that one little sentimental patch unquilted."

In 1969, the first magazine devoted solely to quilters and quilt enthusiasts, *Quilter's Newsletter*, was started by Bonnie Leman at her kitchen table. The first book about quilting is generally considered to be *The Romance of the Patchwork Quilt* by Carrie A. Hall and Rose G. Kretsinger, published in 1935.

Whether *Quiltfolk* is a book or a magazine is a question that comes up a lot, especially when people see the publication for the first time. The heft of it, the quality of our stories and photography, and the blessed absence of ads lead them to exclaim, "Oh, it's a book!"

The truth is, *Quiltfolk* is closer to being a magazine. Consider that we publish quarterly. We take location trips every season. We run feature articles on a variety of quilt-related subjects for each issue, and we're able to bring you exceptional, current content — all of which tip us into the magazine zone even with our book-like characteristics.

This groovy hybrid model poses challenges, though. Page limits, rolling press deadlines, a tight budget — we must respect these magazine boundaries while doing our utmost to bring you book-like quality four times per year. This makes my job as editor in chief both tough and thrilling: While I can't commission a writer to develop a book about *only* Gwen Marston, I can facilitate a feature story that celebrates the legendary Michigander's life in a few gorgeous pages. Maybe that's why I love magazine publishing so much: that intensity can produce a stellar reading experience you can enjoy in the time it takes to sip a cup of tea.

Which brings me to Michigan.

Michigan, in case you didn't know, is very beautiful, tall as it is wide, and saturated with quilters and quilt history. I was struck by how connected Michigan quilters are to one another. Often, the quilter interviewed in the afternoon had a close relationship to the quilter we had interviewed that morning. This tight-knit community, found across the grand, natural beauty of Michigan, was inspiring to the whole *Quiltfolk* team.

We are deeply grateful to the good quilters of Michigan for opening their lives and their work to us for Issue 08. We strived to make it the best issue yet, and I feel we succeeded. Book, magazine, or "bookazine," as one fan recently called it, *Quiltfolk* is the first of its kind. And as long as you enjoy it, you can call it anything you please.

xoxo,

Mary Fons
EDITOR IN CHIEF

Quiltfolk

ISSUE
08

THIS PAGE: A vintage Pinwheel quilt, photographed as the sun sets over a Michigan hay field. **ON THE COVER:** A well-loved Dresden Fan flaps in the breeze at Lynn Carson Harris's farm in Chelsea. Carson Harris's grandmother, Katherine Carson, made the quilt with neighbor and lifelong friend, Margaret Moon. **BACK COVER:** Detail, *Bow Tie* quilt by Mary Schafer (ca. 1982).

08 | *Michigan*

Most quilters are fond of their home state, but Michiganders are positively obsessed with theirs — and you can't blame them. The state has long been a haven for quilters, high-profile and others, whether they made quilts generations ago or are working in their studios right now.

The natural beauty of the state is hard to resist. If a quilt's outermost border is the binding, Michigan's "binding" is water. The Wolverine state touches four out of the five Great Lakes and there's more freshwater shoreline here, mile for mile, than anywhere else in the world. The fields and woods, too, offer places for quilters to flourish. Most of us wouldn't mind a few weeks in one of those famous Michigan cabins, stitching away on our latest project, gazing out the window at the thick trees, listening to birdsong, or maybe catching a deer ambling by.

Of course, Michigan is not all countryside. In East Lansing, 50,000 students flock to MSU each year — and four of the school's quilt-world-famous professors gave us a VIP tour of their singular quilt collection. Several quilt industry celebrities currently call Ann Arbor home, while longtime Flint resident Mary Schafer often comes up in conversation, a decade after her passing. And in "Motor City," quilters are proving that, although Detroit has had its struggles, its beauty is alive and well and stitched in love.

We traveled from the top of Michigan's mitten to its "thumb," from the center of the state down to the southernmost border, to bring you the quilters and quilts of Michigan. Come explore what we found, and get ready: You're about to get a little obsessed with Michigan too. 📿

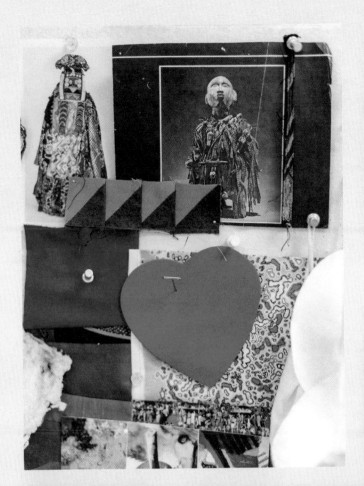

UP NORTH

Where Quilters Take Flight

UP NORTH

TO BE "UP NORTH" IN MICHIGAN is to find extra helpings of the state's natural beauty. Between the Upper Peninsula (the "UP") and the northern area considered the "top of the mitten," there's more shoreline, forest, wildlife, and clean, fresh air to take in. Perhaps the region's natural splendor feels all the more dramatic because of what the place doesn't have much of: people.

But there are those who make their home in the rugged region — quilters included. A dozen guilds dot the area, from Charlevoix to Marquette to Traverse City, all welcoming members who may have to drive long distances to attend meetings and events.

Quilt blocks and quilt patterns here channel the landscape of Northern Michigan. Quilters make use of traditional blocks like Bear Tracks, Constellation, or Tree Everlasting to communicate their environment through fabric.

The quilters we met up north — including living legend Gwen Marston; two-time heavyweight quilt champ Ann Loveless; and quilt scholar Rachel May who wrote a groundbreaking new book — have taken those traditional cues into their studios and studies and pushed them forward. Like setting sail into one of the Great Lakes, quilters in the north of Michigan set out where the air is clear.

BY **Meg Cox**

Rachel May

HISTORY, PIECE BY PIECE

———

Much of the Upper Peninsula of Michigan is wild and remote. The average annual snowfall for the region is 152 feet, and winter can last up to eight months. Immigrants from Finland, French Canada, and Sweden have heavily influenced the culture and language and every so often the residents of the UP, who call themselves "yoopers," threaten to secede from Michigan and form a new state called "Superior."

It is fair to say that quilt historian and author Rachel May suffered some culture shock when she moved here in 2015 to become an assistant professor at Northern Michigan University, based in the region's largest city, Marquette. She found the locals to be "quirky," generally passionate about hunting (there's a gun storage room on campus), and extremely friendly. For someone who grew up in Boston and lived in New England in recent years, all of this took some getting used to.

Writer, quilter, and historian Rachel May with an early draft of her critically acclaimed book, *An American Quilt: Unfolding a Story of Family and Slavery.*

ABOVE: Modern-style patchwork by May, a founding member of the Boston Modern Quilt Guild. **OPPOSITE:** The air in Michigan's Upper Peninsula helps a scholar like May clear her head.

"Friends who went to NMU had told me how beautiful it is in the UP, but I never expected to live here," said May. When she began looking for a teaching job after acquiring her PhD and the college called her to interview, she considered it "kismet." She's now happily ensconced in a tenure-track position that allows her to teach both undergraduate and graduate students, primarily in nonfiction writing. "I've always loved the snow and my dog loves it too," May said. She is hoping to raise chickens in her backyard soon. And now she owns special cross-country skis that let her explore the deep woods.

May, who is now 41 years old, was a writer long before she was a quilter, but she's been able to combine both passions lately. Her first published book explored the roots of modern quilting and came out in 2014, and her recently published book *An American Quilt: Unfolding a Story of Family and Slavery* (2018) grew out of May's scholarly life.

May made her first quilt in graduate school, about 10 years ago, when a friend was getting married and May decided to make a quilt as her wedding gift. Her sewing in those days had mostly consisted of very small projects like bags, until she decided to continue her graduate school education back east.

The winter she arrived in Providence, Rhode Island, the Boston Modern Quilt Guild was just starting up, and Rachel May became a founding member. "About 30 of us met at a little fabric shop. The women were about my age and we all became such good friends. I loved the community," said May. "I was so happy to find people who loved to sew and didn't judge me for the awful quilts I was making at the time. They taught me how to make bindings and match points and all the stuff I couldn't figure out on my own."

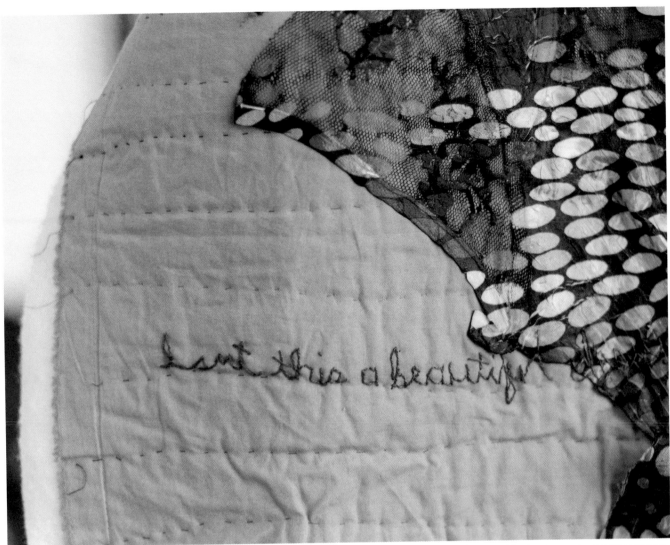

ABOVE, OPPOSITE: Today, May works exclusively with fabrics she already owns or with reclaimed vintage blocks. A meaningful dress from a different season in May's life serves as the basis for this art quilt.

She kept telling the group she thought there was a book in this new movement, and when an editor from Storey Publishing came to one of the guild's meetings, May got a chance to pitch the idea for what became *Quilting with a Modern Slant: People, Patterns, and Techniques Inspiring the Modern Quilt Community.* The 2014 book garnered rave reviews by *Library Journal* and the *Los Angeles Times*; was called the "seminal" work on the modern movement by prominent quilt designer Weeks Ringle; and sold 15,000 copies.

As a writer and a quilter, Rachel May loves to "cross genre boundaries." She doesn't consider herself strictly a modern quilter but rather an art quilter. In a book of fiction fragments called *The Experiments* that May published in 2015, the illustrations are photographs of appliquéd fabric collages she made. Much of her writing is also hybrid in nature, including *Quilting with a Modern Slant*, which combines dozens of profiles of notable designers with tutorials and historical background about what influenced the founders of the modern quilt movement.

But by far, the biggest and most impressive genre-crossing project of May's career to date is her new book, *An American Quilt: Unfolding a Story of Family and Slavery.* This is a well-researched book that uses one family's story, uncovered thanks to several unfinished quilts, to delve into a consequential look at slavery in America.

The germ of the story began in graduate school in Providence, where May was taking a class in

ABOVE: To write *An American Quilt*, May pored over hundreds of documents such as marriage records, death notices, and handwritten letters like this one. **OPPOSITE:** Now that the book is finished, May hopes to finish this vintage Snowball quilt top

material culture. As part of that course, she was given three unfinished vintage quilts to examine, made from paper-pieced hexagons whose yellowed papers were still intact, though fragile, on the backside. She was thrilled to see and touch these nearly 200-year-old quilt tops. All the university seemed to know was that the tops were stitched by a newlywed couple in Charleston, South Carolina, in the 1830s. The tops had been kept in a trunk that was donated to the school by a relative in the 1950s.

May spent weeks poring over the fabrics in the tops and began examining the bits of old letters, sheet music, and bills with dates as old as 1798 that were stuck in the backs of the hexagons. Her professor told her that the quilt tops came with two journals that she could study as well. What was

supposed to be a one-semester study gradually came to dominate May's imagination and become a years-long project.

In the journals, references to the family's slaves quickly fascinated May. The wife in the couple, Susan, was from Providence, but she had married Hasell Crouch and gone to live with his family in Charleston, South Carolina. "Why did Susan [...] wind up moving South and owning slaves? Why was she OK with that?" said May. She began to learn more about the family's slaves — including Minerva, Jane, and Juba, the cook — and wanted to understand what it was like to be an enslaved person in Charleston at that time.

May went to great lengths to follow the threads of this story, eventually creating an elaborate paper

ABOVE, OPPOSITE: To weave the tale of *An American Quilt*, May painstakingly reconstructed the story's timeline.

timeline that placed incidents of the Crouch family history into the context of the country's laws and events. She took a research trip to Charleston in 2014 and later hired a genealogist to learn more about the family's slaves and attempt to find their descendants. Then, May discovered a cache of family letters at the Rhode Island Historical Society — hundreds of them — making the story even stronger.

Susan and Hasell, who are said to have designed and sewn the oldest quilt top and made hexagons for the other two, were connected to some of the major issues and people of the day: for example, Susan's brother sold cotton from plantation owners in the South to mill owners in the North. So May decided to write about how industrialization and slavery were codependent. "The cotton boom helped fuel the building of the textile mills, and then we needed more slaves to pick more cotton for free," said May. "Even abolitionists in the North were invested in those mills." With diligent digging, May discovered what happened to the Crouch family's slaves after Hasell died and Susan moved back up north: The slaves were resold, and some were freed after the Civil War.

Rachel May's brilliant storytelling is what makes *An American Quilt* so compelling. She guides us through her discoveries and thought process, and we see her try to wrap her 21st-century mind around these 19th-century lives and morals.

"I struggle to let go of these people from the past," she writes at the end. She may not have gotten all the answers she sought, but May used her scholarship and compassion to shine a bright light on a difficult history, led by quilts.

BY **Meg Cox**

Gwen Marston
HER OWN FINE SELF

To reach Gwen Marston's rustic home on Michigan's Beaver Island, you either need to take a two-hour ferry ride or a 15-minute flight in the sort of propeller plane often dubbed a puddle jumper. But in this case, the "puddle" you're jumping over is Lake Michigan. Only 600 people live year-round on this thickly wooded, pear-shaped island, 55 square miles dotted with seven small lakes.

The house echoes Marston's characteristic style of quiltmaking: simple, clean lines that cohere into a powerful image of spare beauty. That aesthetic and her improvisational techniques for achieving it made her one of the most sought-after and influential quilt teachers in the country. But last year, at 80, Marston retired from all that.

When we met her, Marston's warm presence felt outsize, bigger than her small, slender frame. She was dressed in jeans and a black long-sleeved T-shirt, having come to the small airfield to meet the *Quiltfolk* team in her weathered red pickup truck. Her trademark bob with even bangs is now gray streaked with white. A mischievous smile lifted her prominent cheekbones.

The incomparable Gwen Marston at home on Beaver Island.

ABOVE: In Marston's second-floor studio, inspiration and supplies abound. **OPPOSITE:** Marston shows one of 10 "color studies" made in 2015. Each quilt measures 33 by 33 inches with allover, straight-line quilting.

Sitting at a table in her living room overlooking the woods and her barely tamed flower garden, Marston said one of the things she loves most about living here is the lack of distraction: she got rid of her TV and doesn't own a cellphone because there is no cell service on the island. During her peak travel and teaching years, she was on the road at least half the year. Otherwise, she was here working in her upstairs windowed studio.

There is a disciplined spareness to the studio. Marston made neat piles of recent work to show the *Quiltfolk* crew and immediately pointed out her beloved sewing machine, a cast-iron workhorse, the Singer 201, that she's used to piece all her quilts. Despite the decades-long trend toward machine-quilting, Marston has famously preferred to hand-quilt her quilts, using a large, adjustable wooden frame.

About that frame: Marston had been trying to learn quilting on her own without success until she came across a group of Mennonite quilters in 1976 in Oregon, where her family was living. The patient women taught her to hand-quilt on this sturdy frame, which is adjusted to a progressively smaller size with the quilt rolled underneath as the quilting is completed.

As the years went by, Marston observed that most quilters switched to machine-quilting but the frame still made the most sense to her: "It's an amazingly simple and effective system," she explained. "Having the quilt stretched out tight [...] guaranteed the quilts would be perfectly square and flat and have no puckers. Plus, you didn't have to baste the layers together, a thankless task." But she recognized that many women don't have the luxury of a large quilting studio like hers, where a frame can stay up as long as needed.

ABOVE: To keep line and form clearly defined in her quilts, Marston turns to solids almost exclusively. **OPPOSITE:** Never pretentious, Marston used her toes to point out a detail for our photographer.

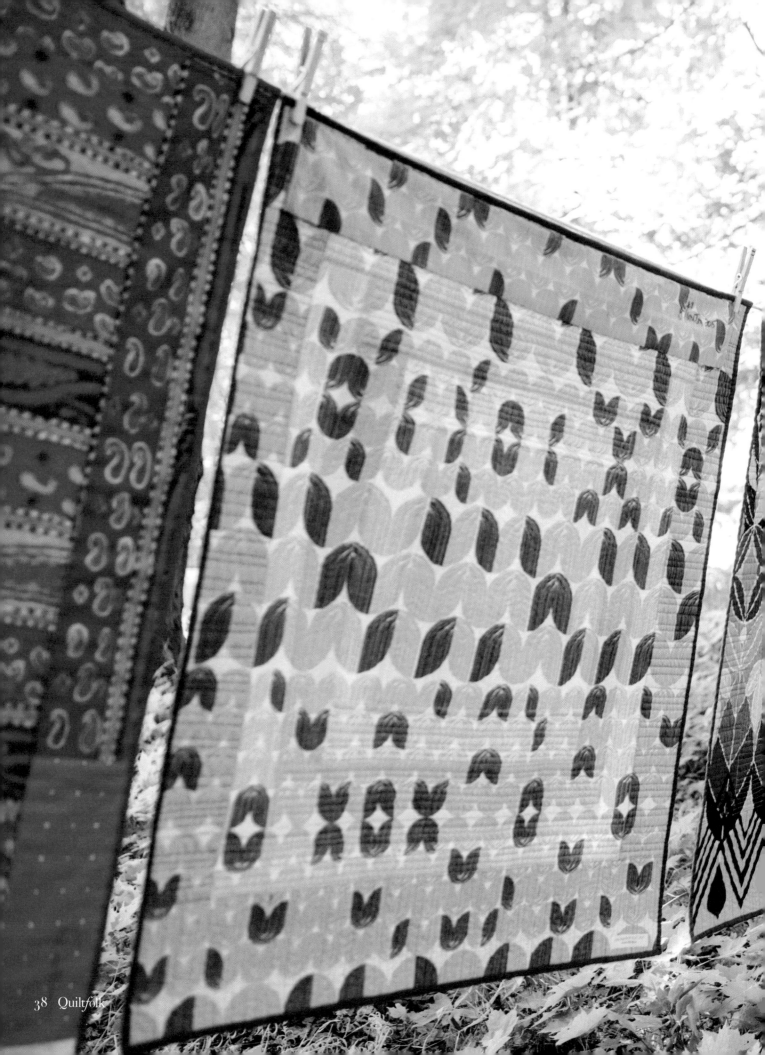

ABOVE: Detail, quilt backs. **PREVIOUS PAGE:** Together, the backs of Marston's 10 quilts tell a story all their own.

Even Marston's iron of choice isn't contemporary: Instead of the fancy, lightweight irons marketed to quilters now, she prefers a 40-year-old model that would break a toe if dropped but presses beautifully and doesn't turn off automatically.

It's hard to believe that someone working in such an antiquated way became the darling of modern quilters. After decades of popularity and several dozen published books, Marston was "discovered" by a new generation.

In 2010, shortly after the Modern Quilt Guild was formed, Marston published an updated version of her 1997 classic book *Liberated Quiltmaking*. Modern quilters felt instantly at home with her aesthetic, which featured solid fabrics and wonky versions of

vintage blocks like Log Cabins.

Canadian fabric and quilt designer Cheryl Arkison, a leading light on the modern scene, called Marston "my personal hero." When a quilt mentor of Arkison's encouraged her to try techniques from the *Liberated Quiltmaking* book, "The heavens parted and the angels started singing," she said. "Suddenly I could see all the possibilities. And I've never stopped improvising."

Marston gave many modern quilters obsessed with precision piecing permission to loosen up and improvise by touting a method that still required precision in other areas. Arkinson remembers the stir Marston created as the keynote speaker at QuiltCon in 2016. "Quilters new to improv are

always shocked when I say that we will still use quarter-inch seam allowances, we will still press our work, and squaring is important [so] that your quilt stays together and lays flat. As the QuiltCon headliner, Gwen said pretty much that same thing and [...] the gasp in the ballroom was audible," said Arkinson. "She made improv obtainable to those who'd never considered it."

Marston has been an inspiration to countless quilters, as she keeps paying forward the greatest lessons from her own mentor, Mary Schafer *(see page 130)*. Schafer was an influential quilter who collected antique quilts starting in the 1950s. Well before the Bicentennial, Schafer was responsible for reviving interest in quilts through her careful scholarship and industriousness in reproducing old quilts. The two women met in the 1970s and Marston helped promote Schafer's work.

While soaking up Schafer's deep knowledge of old quilts, Marston came to a revelation that shocked her. "I could see mounting evidence that many early quiltmakers were not following arbitrary rules nor were they using patterns. They were figuring things out for themselves, which resulted in innovation and originality in their work." When the quilt revival began in the 1970s and quilters started slavishly following patterns and teachers, Marston went another way. "I made an abrupt left turn and figured out how to make quilts that echoed the freedom and spontaneity found in old quilts."

ABOVE: Marston's twin habits of being methodical and practical guide her process. **OPPOSITE:** *The Magic Forest,* Marston's latest book, features 31 appliquéd tree quilts, each with a complementary poem, proverb, or haiku.

Being both methodical and practical are constant themes in Marston's work and allure. For 30 years she hosted an annual retreat on Beaver Island and, because many people came annually, she changed the theme every single year. She would pick a theme, say Flower Basket blocks or string quilts, and spend the entire year researching it. By then, she'd have enough material for a book on that block or theme: Thirty-one Gwen Marston books have been published over the years.

Marston's resilient practicality helped her to adapt techniques as she aged. After 50 years of hand-quilting, her hands are "giving me trouble," she said, so she decided to experiment with machine-quilting on her vintage Singer. "You can't lower the feed dogs and I used no special feet," she said. "But I loved the effect. The thread gets pulled a little as you quilt the straight lines and that ended up creating a herringbone effect. I've spent my whole life avoiding puckers, and now I embrace them."

What will her legacy be in the end? Marston said she doesn't read quilt magazines or keep up with the quilt world online. But what she fervently hopes is that her many books and years of teaching will continue to liberate quilters in more than one way.

If she does have a complaint about how quilting has changed, Marston feels that it's gone too commercial and quilters have become too reliant on patterns. "It's all about celebrity and about patterns. You can't make a simple Four Patch these days without a pattern," she said. "So many teachers just teach their quilt step by step. [...] What I hope is that people will find their own tack, their own way of doing things. Then, their work has a chance to really stand out."

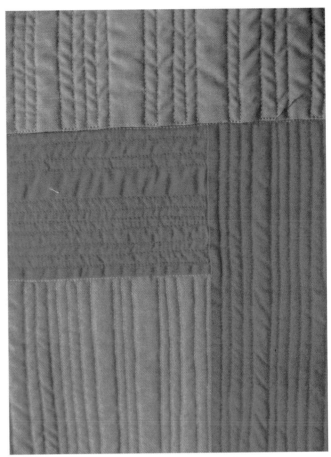

ABOVE: Saturated color — a Marston hallmark. **OPPOSITE:** The artist in her studio, happy to keep company with her own fine self.

"I've spent my whole life avoiding puckers, and now I embrace them."

— GWEN MARSTON

One thing is for sure: Gwen Marston made a career out of doing things her own way and she won't stop now.

Last winter was the first Marston has spent here since retirement, cocooned in her house, toasty warm from her wood-burning stove. She broke up the stretch of isolation with some visits to family, including her London-based songwriter son. But she relished the time alone, digging into the high stack of poetry books on her bedside table and the weighty nonfiction tomes she'd long wanted to read.

"I would get up when it was still dark, press the button on my coffee maker, and sit in this comfortable chair in the living room, watching the light come up," she recalled. "And I thought, you've never had the time to just sit quietly with your own fine self. That's where you make discoveries!"

Marston doesn't expect to feel lonely, especially during the warmer parts of the year. Her compact, modern guest house will be filled with a succession of friends and family. In truth, Marston doesn't have a set plan or expectations for what she'll do with this next gift of time. She isn't even sure how much of it will include quilting, although she finally got the chance to complete a brightly colored Pinwheel quilt for her grandson.

"I've had ever so many people come up to me with a furrowed brow and say, 'But what will you do?'" Marston said. "I've never been bored for a minute of my life. I just look forward to living life fully. Quilting just developed all on its own, and I like to do life that way."

"FEATHERWEIGHT MONTE" EXPLAINS IT ALL

In 1934, in the depths of the Great Depression, the Singer Manufacturing Company introduced a new product at the Chicago World's Fair. "The Singer Featherweight model 221," said Monte Graham, looking lovingly at the sleek black machine in front of him. "And it was one of the greatest inventions of the 20th century."

Sure, the jolly Featherweight technician, historian, and general fanatic is biased — he and wife Carol have 50 of the machines in their collection — but he's not wrong. The 11-pound Singer, with its electric motor and extended swinging bed (what most now call an "apron"), ushered in a new dawn in home sewing for untold numbers of women in the US and beyond. "Most people could afford one, since you could pay installments," Graham said. "It was [one of] the first installment plans in the country. Isn't that cool?"

It was endearing how many times Graham said "Isn't that cool?" when discussing his favorite topic. And his topic *is* cool: Singer's first electric sewing machines each have their own fascinating stats (did you know a rare "Crinkle" model in perfect condition can sell as high as $5,000?); each machine has its own place in American history (no machines were made from 1942 to 1945, so the chromium could go into World War II gun barrels instead); and each has

its own individual provenance — which is sometimes a head scratcher.

"We had a machine come in once that had chicken feathers in it," Carol said, shaking her head. But then her husband piped up. "You can fix pretty much anything! These babies are almost indestructible." Is there *anything* that takes a Featherweight out for good? The man in the suspenders blinked. "Salt water in the motor," he said. "That's bad."

Anyone who doesn't get why people go gaga over what Singer dubbed its "Perfect Portable" need only spend an hour with this Featherweight power couple — and at gorgeous Bittersweet Quilt Shop and Home Décor in Pinconning, Michigan, you can. Eight years ago, owner Tina Bauer, whose distinctive shop has been featured in *Better Homes and Gardens*, welcomed Monte "into the family" as her Featherweight service man. Once a month, Bittersweet hosts a Featherweight clinic in the basement, where anyone can come in for service questions on their 221s and 301s (Monte's speciality) and learn the history of these small-but-mighty machines from two Michiganders who can't get enough of them.

"People come from all over for the clinic," said Bauer. "They come in because they're interested in the machines, but then they just fall in love with Monte." Bauer patted his arm. "We sure did."

FROM LEFT: Housed in a former church, Bittersweet Quilt Shop and Home Décor is heaven for quilters; Singer ephemera from the Grahams' collection; Carol and Monte in Pinconning.

BY **Mary Fons**

Ann Loveless
THE ARTIST NEXT DOOR

It's a typical story, really: Girl grows up in Michigan. Girl gets good at sewing. Girl raises family. Girl enters quilt in world's largest public art competition and wins $200,000 and trophy for first place.

Twice.

So maybe Ann Loveless's story isn't typical. But to look at the lifelong Frankfort resident, with her sensible haircut and a touch of that "yooper" accent, you'd never guess that her journey with a needle and thread plunked her directly into the center of the complicated, ongoing debate: Are quilts art?

Loveless and her husband and collaborator, Steve, just let folks duke it out. The couple are more than happy to continue doing what they love in their small Michigan town, quietly making a fine place for themselves in the world of textile art, one quilt at a time.

For quilt artist Ann Loveless, the beauty of Michigan is in the details.

At home with Ann

Anyone who visits Northern Michigan will encounter gorgeous scenery. Maybe you catch the sun setting over a beach in summer; maybe you spy a cardinal alighting on a snow-capped tree in winter. Whatever the season, Michigan scenery tends to inspire even the least artistically inclined among us. Thankfully, artists like Loveless have the vision, the talent, and the chops to translate those singular Michigan views into something you might actually want to hang on a wall in your house. And since Loveless prefers to work with a sewing machine, quilters have even more reason to applaud her success.

Loveless is no stranger to applause. The mother of three stood on stage to thunderous cheers for winning first place at ArtPrize in 2013. Any artist, working in any medium, can enter the art competition, which takes place each fall in Grand Rapids, Michigan. Some 300,000 people visit the ArtPrize festival each year, and they have a say in what happens: An expert jury panel awards a $200,000 prize, but the public gets to award a cool $200,000 prize too. In 2013, Loveless's panoramic art quilt, *Sleeping Bear Dune Lakeshore* (5 by 20 feet), was chosen by the audience as Best in Show. *Sleeping Bear Dune Lakeshore* was the first quilt to win ArtPrize; it set a record for the most prize money ever awarded to a quilt.

Whatever their medium, artists would have a tough time following up such a win. "It doesn't get much better than that,'" Loveless said. "Winning ArtPrize brought so many new opportunities to teach and sell my work, so I was just happy to have that." When her daughter suggested that she enter again, this time in collaboration with husband Steve, a professional photographer, the champ thought, "What's the worst that could happen?"

In fact, the *best* thing that could happen did: Ann and Steve won ArtPrize *again* in 2015. Their hybrid photo-textile panorama, *Northwood Awakening* (5 by 25 feet), bagged them another first-place trophy, another check for almost a quarter of a million dollars, and another round of celebration, accolades, and opportunity knocking.

Did she and Steve buy a private island? Did they at least go to Disney World? "No," Loveless laughed. "Nothing like that. We set up college funds for our grandkids. I guess I did buy a new car, but it's just a Jeep."

The win came with a lot of publicity, but not all of it was positive. "There was one article where the guy couldn't get over a quilt winning," Loveless said. "He said they should change the name of ArtPrize to 'CraftPrize.' That was a low." The accolades far outweighed the criticism, though, and sewists everywhere were thrilled. "All the quilters were like, 'Go Ann!'" Loveless smiled.

OPPOSITE: The Lovelesses' cottage has been in Ann's family for four generations — five, if you count Peter the dog.

ABOVE: Loveless starts work early in her spacious, sun-lit studio. **OPPOSITE:** Detail, a work in progress.

Portrait of the artist as a quilter

To watch Loveless work on one of her impressionistic landscape quilts in her sunny studio is to witness a kind of alchemy: a photograph becomes a textile, then somehow becomes a photograph again — only now rendered in fabric. Working from wide-angle shots of mostly natural landscapes taken by Steve, Loveless fuses thousands of tiny pieces of fabric into a given work before it gets free-motion-quilted at her domestic sewing machine or her Handi Quilter longarm. The finished piece may be as small as 4 by 6 inches or as large as *Northwood Awakening*. Whatever the size, Loveless works with effortless efficiency, understanding at a glance what tones she'll need to create the scene before her.

"I want to get some lightness in here that kind of takes your eye back in," she said, letting a pale green chip of fabric flutter into place. It's all intuitive for this self-described quilt artist. "I don't do any patterns or tracing. I just like to make it up as I go." She grinned. "I was bad about following directions as a kid."

Loveless followed directions well enough, however, to earn a degree in Apparel and Textile Design at Michigan State University (MSU), taking classes in art history, drawing, and color theory. Today, her medium is mostly quilter's cotton, but when working with her collage technique, she'll use other textiles such as upholstery fabrics, wool, and yarn to get texture.

CLOCKWISE FROM UPPER LEFT: Once the fabrics have been placed, the quilting begins; the artist's free-motion signature; Loveless keeps herself busy, working on multiple projects simultaneously.

ABOVE: Artistic power couple Steve and Ann Loveless at their shop, State of the Art Framing and Gallery in Beulah.

Loveless says she can whip out one of her smallest works in a few hours; the piece she demonstrated for us when we arrived had been started at 7:30 that morning. She has no choice but to work quickly: These mini-quilts sell at a steady clip at the gallery she and her husband own in nearby Beulah. When we visited State of the Art Framing and Gallery, Steve Loveless led us into the room almost entirely dedicated to selling the couple's work. A number of guests perused Ann's fabric pieces and Steve's panoramic prints.

Will the Michigan power couple go for the triple crown and win at ArtPrize just one more time? "Well, after the 2015 win, they changed the rules," Ann Loveless said. "If you win ArtPrize once, you can't win first place again, and I understand why. The competition is about supporting artists, so it doesn't make sense to have the same person win over and over."

For now, the Lovelesses are looking forward, not back. Ann is getting teaching offers from guilds all over the country; she's doing multiple commissions every year; and she published a book about her techniques. Next summer, the couple will host their first retreat in Frankfort for those wanting to spend a week at the lake learning from the unlikely art world celebrities.

"We're excited to host the retreats," Ann Loveless said. "It's amazing what people can do in classes, and I do think I bring out their creativity. Everybody's artistic, we just don't give ourselves enough credit." Perhaps Loveless's success — and a little time spent in beautiful Michigan — will bring out the artist in us all.

OH, FAIR PENINSULA

The Thumb of Michigan's "Mitten"

FIFTH THIRD BANK

OH, FAIR PENINSULA

DUE TO ITS UNIQUE SHAPE, Michigan is known as the Mitten State. Its "thumb" is a peninsula featuring miles of forest, shoreline, and beaches. But the region is also an American industrial leviathan. Henry Ford, William Durant, Thomas Edison, and many other innovators changed how each one of us lives today — and they did their groundbreaking work in Michigan.

Quilts were there all along, of course. When you think about the output of quilts around the turn of the century, you can't help but wonder if there were as many quilts made in America as there were cars coming out of Detroit. At The Henry Ford in Dearborn, we found hundreds of examples of patchwork and appliqué. And a lover of cars and quilts in Auburn Hills treated us to a look at her collection, provoking a surprising conversation about the similarities between classic cars and classic quilts.

Quilts of all sorts, from "fancy" to plain, cover Michigan's Blue Water Area. World-renowned art quilter Carole Harris looks out on her beloved Detroit as she works in her studio; Joanne Dotson is painting quilt blocks for use on barns in Michigan and beyond; and quilt superstar sisters are stitching another masterpiece. The quilters on the "thumb" of Michigan are doing some powerful lifting.

BY **Laura McDowell Hopper**

Pass It On

GREAT LAKES AFRICAN AMERICAN QUILTERS' NETWORK

"I joined for the sisterhood," said April Shipp, vice president of the Great Lakes African American Quilters' Network (GLAAQN). "If I've got a problem, I call my sisters. [...] It's my quilt family." *Quiltfolk* met with nine leaders and board members of this 122-member quilt family and learned about their history and passions — and their version of *Project Runway*.

Founded in 2002, GLAAQN aimed to create an information network to connect African American quilters, particularly around Detroit. They've worked toward that goal through charity quilting, giving back to the community, and preserving and writing their own history.

Guild president and longtime quilter, the warm-hearted Sharon Ray.

THIS PAGE, OPPOSITE: Details from a few members' quilts show the skill, style, and passion present in the Network.

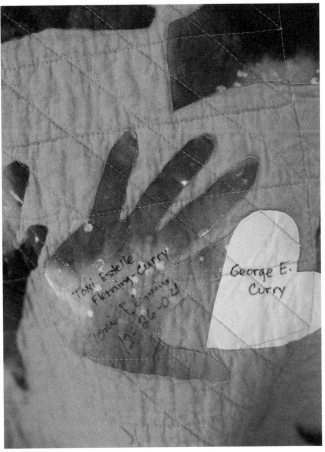

ABOVE: Members of GLAAQN at the Charles H. Wright Museum of African American History. **OPPOSITE, FROM LEFT:** Carolyn Bunkley, Sharon Ray, Kaye Whittington, April Shipp, Linda Ali, Karla Middlebrooks, Pat Murphy, Wanda Nash, and Theadra Fleming near Detroit artist Charles McGee's *United We Stand* sculpture.

Today, the Network is led by President Sharon Ray. "It's a passion that you have to have, not just for quilting but also for what it means to the community," Ray said. Members meet each month, alternating between regular meetings and classes. "We talk about general business. [...] Then we have *Project Runway*."

Unlike the television show, GLAAQN doesn't require members to do sewing challenges for prizes. "At first, show-and-tell was so dull," Shipp said, "and I thought, let's spice it up. We make everyone get their quilt and sashay down the aisle with pride. If you took the time to sew it, be proud of [it]." Sometimes they play the soundtrack to *Soul Train* as members walk the "catwalk." "The first time I attended, [...] I was intimidated," member Pat Murphy said. "Everybody kept saying, 'Come back,' and I just fell in love."

GLAAQN members know how to have a good time and they bring this energy to the annual African World Festival at the Charles H. Wright Museum of African American History, where the GLAAQN tent is dedicated to teaching Detroiters about quilting. Activities include quilting demonstrations, paper quilt crafts for kids, and a pop-up exhibit of GLAAQN quilts in the museum's rotunda.

The group is planning something special for their activities at the festival in August. "We are purchasing ten sewing machines to have free classes for three days," said Carolyn Bunkley, who heads up the volunteer team. GLAAQN members, with help from a local quilt shop, have donated supplies for free kits so that class attendees have all they need to make their first quilt. "It's our passion that people learn to quilt, continue to quilt, and pass it on to their families," Bunkley said.

GLAAQN was founded to unite African American quilters around Detroit. Now its members want to inspire others in the city to fall in love with quilting. And if anyone can inspire, it's these passionate, talented, and fun-loving women.

BY **Meg Cox**

Hard Work, Soft Quilts

EXPLORING THE HENRY FORD

Born on a farm in Michigan three weeks after the Battle of Gettysburg, Henry Ford became famous for launching the age of mass production and consumption. His Ford Model T first appeared in 1908: A decade later, half the cars in America were Model Ts.

The Henry Ford in Dearborn, Michigan, a vast museum and monument to the man's genius, is full of classic cars and "oh wow" machines of every sort. But another passion defined Henry Ford: a deep respect for doing practical work with one's hands. In his teens, Ford made extra money by repairing watches, going so far as to invent his own tools for doing so. While other rich men of his time collected art, Ford wanted to fill a museum with the humble objects that proved the ingenuity, resourcefulness, and innovation of everyday Americans. According to Jeanine Head Miller, curator of Domestic Life at The Henry Ford, quilts were "among some of his first acquisitions."

At The Henry Ford, a full-service 1940s diner serves true-to-period breakfast, lunch, and dinner.

ABOVE, FROM LEFT: An "exploded" Model T shows the simplicity and genius of the car's design; in the quilt and textile collections room, fabric swatches from the 19th century. **OPPOSITE:** Miller offers a peek at a quilt by Susana Allen Hunter.

Today, in a collection of more than one million objects that include everything from a Ford Model A owned by Thomas Edison to one of the first Apple-1 computers built in 1976 and the bus in which Rosa Parks refused to give up her seat, there are 330 quilts.

"I think part of why Ford collected objects of everyday life in the home, such as quilts and cooking tools, is that they were an emotional touchstone for him," Miller said. "He was about 13 when his mother died from complications of childbirth. He later moved and restored his childhood home [to prevent it being razed when a road was built] as a kind of memorial to his mother."

As a quilter herself, curator Miller couldn't help getting a little emotional as she revealed some of the museum's greatest treasures to the *Quiltfolk* team. Opening a series of shallow drawers within a vast room that is climate-controlled and locked, as museum protocol demands, she explained that the collection includes quilts from the early 18th

century to the 21st century, gathered from all over the country. Henry Ford died before the museum began collecting the quilts of a 19th-century Indiana housewife named Susan McCord, but her wildly original designs exhibit the resourcefulness he celebrated so fiercely.

Like many museums that collect quilts, The Henry Ford is no longer interested in presenting quilts with vague labels that read, "This is a typical example of such-and-such pattern." To enter this collection now, Miller said, quilts must have a compelling story to tell, especially in the context of the museum's collection and mission.

One of the quilts she pulled out for *Quiltfolk* was made by a woman who bestows one each year upon the winner of the Indianapolis 500: The museum has hundreds of artifacts related to the Indy 500, including vintage race cars. Miller mentioned that the collection includes quilts people gave to the museum or to Henry Ford himself, often in gratitude for his practical cars. "One young woman sent a

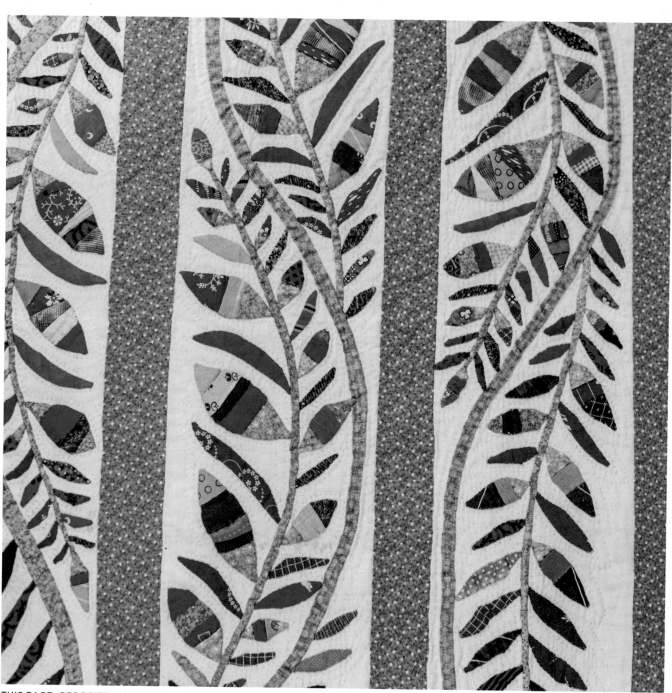

THIS PAGE, OPPOSITE: When Susan McCord's well-known *Vine Quilt* (ca. 1880-1890) was revealed, audible gasps filled the room.
PREVIOUS PAGE: The singular *Fan Variation Quilt* (ca. 1900) is one of many McCord pieces now preserved at The Henry Ford.

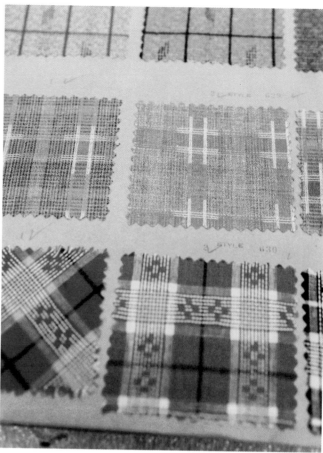

CLOCKWISE FROM UPPER LEFT: Iconic cars in the museum's "Driving America" exhibit; a fabric merchant's swatch card; blue jeans incorporated into a quilt by Susana Allen Hunter.

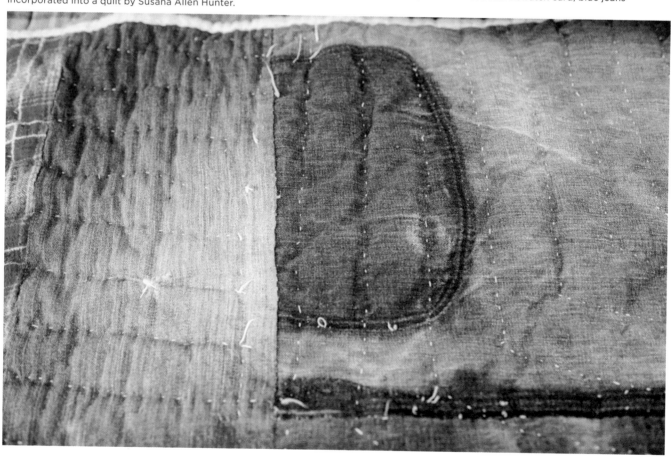

Spotted in a display of domestic artifacts, this unusual-looking sewing machine suggests a different time for sewists.

gorgeous Wedding Ring quilt, which she said was her first," said Miller. "She keeps talking in her letter about how much she loves the Ford cars, and it seems clear she is hoping Henry Ford will send her a free car."

Miller is especially proud of a collection of 34 quilts made by African American quilter Susana Allen Hunter. Hunter lived in Wilcox County, Alabama, from 1912 to 2005, not far from Gee's Bend. Miller said Hunter made hundreds of quilts, generally improvisational works that included materials from her husband's work shirts and feedsacks.

The quilter's husband is said to have complained to his wife, "You quilt too much!" The museum knows this because they've been able to interview members of the extended family and acquire everyday household items that Hunter used, including a bucket she would carry to the well, a half mile

away from her home. Henry Ford would definitely have approved.

In a collection famous for hard machines, Miller hopes the public doesn't miss these soft textiles that also tell the stories of their times. "I would love for people to know that we have this fabulous quilt collection and I would like them to understand how incredibly rich the collection is in variety."

While the quilts are rarely on display, more than 120 of the most glorious and significant pieces can be seen and studied by going to The Henry Ford's excellent digital collection. And if you want to try your hand at making some of the museum's most popular quilts, including two by Susan McCord, you can still find copies of a 2005 book by Marianne Fons and Liz Porter called *Quilts from The Henry Ford*, which includes patterns and directions for a few of the museum's masterpieces.

CLASSIC CARS, CLASSIC QUILTS

What do classic cars and classic quilts have in common?
Detroit-area quilter and car aficionado Karen Lieberman explores the idea.

My parents are collectors of fine art and antiques. At 15, I started working for my mother at antique shows and conducting estate sales. It was a wonderful education that created my desire to collect and preserve pieces from the past.

My grandmother introduced me to needlework, teaching me to crochet when I was just five years old. When I was 13, I told my mom how much I loved sewing in home ec, so she took me to Sears and bought me a sewing machine. A year later, I made my first quilt, and I've been making them for the past 42 years.

The same year I made my first quilt, I met my future husband, Mark. We started dating at 16. We both had a passion for cars; growing up in the metro Detroit area, you can't help but have an appreciation for automobiles. When our friends were getting jobs at restaurants or at the mall, Mark and I were buying cars to fix up and sell. We were married the summer we turned 18 and went off to college together. Today, we run a classic and exotic car dealership. We love all aspects of the classic car hobby: buying, selling, collecting, restoring, and showing.

There are many similarities between what we look for in a classic car and a classic quilt: Where and when was it made? Who designed it? How did culture affect the design or materials used? Do new innovations from the era, such as dyes or software, show up in the work? Did the maker(s) win any awards? How popular has the "model" been over the years? Both cars and quilts have stories to tell based on their history.

OPPOSITE: Lieberman with a silk Log Cabin quilt top and a 1948 Tucker.

ABOVE: A vintage Crazy quilt, made by Lieberman's grandmother and her cousin, complements a 1966 Mustang like the one Lieberman drove in high school. **OPPOSITE:** A silk Log Cabin top is right at home on the seat of Tucker #29, the personal car of automobile entrepreneur Preston Tucker.

When researching cars, you have titles, build sheets, service records, and other data available; quilts can be much trickier. Experts can look at designs, date fabrics, and hopefully track down genealogy records, but nothing beats having information embroidered on a quilt. It's so important for quilters today to label our quilts, to satisfy the curiosity of tomorrow's collectors.

I've noticed a similar trend in the realms of the quilt and the car: Classics are being redesigned and reimagined in exciting ways. Manufacturers of the late 1960s Chevy Camaro and early 1970s Dodge Challenger have released new versions of both, and car enthusiasts are loving them. The new designs combine the classic lines and contours of the originals with contemporary features and styling — perfect blends of vintage and modern.

The modern quilt movement has done the same thing with classic vintage quilt designs. Modern quilters are using blocks like Log Cabin and Churn Dash as inspiration and reimagining ways to use them in their art. Fascinating new quilts are being born from the patterns of past eras.

Mark and I still cruise Woodward Avenue on Saturday nights like we did in high school 40 years ago. Sometimes we drive his 1973 red Dodge Challenger or my 1966 yellow Mustang convertible. Driving a classic car gives you a direct connection to the past. Sometimes we take out a 1948 Tucker and imagine what it would have been like to drive around in the 1940s. Sleeping under a vintage quilt feels like a connection to the past too. The same quilt keeping you warm in the suburbs may have kept someone else warm on a farm. Maybe a Victorian Crazy quilt you use as a bedspread was draped over a beautiful sofa in the parlor of a city mansion.

It's fun to imagine what stories your quilts have lived. I believe the need for that connection feeds our passion for collecting, whether your passion is for classic cars or classic quilts — or both.

BY **Laura McDowell Hopper**

Carole Harris
A STAR IN DETROIT

Carole Harris's home studio is filled with piles of fabrics she's collected over the years. *Molas* from Panama, screen-printed activist slogans, scraps from other quilts, and fabrics she has rust-dyed wait patiently to be used. Quilts in progress decorate the studio walls. Harris looks at one and says, "It's mellowing out. I'm letting it talk to me."

Harris's home is a stone's throw away from one of Detroit's greatest artistic landmarks: the Detroit Institute of Art. This museum is home to the *Detroit Industry Murals* by Diego Rivera, *Self-Portrait with a Straw Hat* by Vincent Van Gogh, and the temporary exhibit *Rhythm, Repetition, and Vocab*, Harris's joint show with Detroit painter Allie McGhee. In over fifty years of quilting, Harris has become an artistic jewel of Detroit.

Artist, entrepreneur, and world traveler Carole Harris looks out on her beloved Detroit.

ABOVE: An early Pinwheel quilt got Harris thinking about patchwork possibilities. PREVIOUS PAGE: A fixture in the Detroit art community, Harris has exhibited work at the Smithsonian, the American Folk Art Museum, and the Museum of Arts and Design.

Finding the melody

"I say life began for me in 1966," said Harris. It was the year she graduated from college, married her husband, and made her first quilt. Harris only had enough fabric on hand to make a few blocks that formed the center of her quilt. As she acquired more fabric, she made Pinwheel borders and watched the quilt grow. "I didn't have any vision for that first quilt, I didn't even know what a quilt was yet," Harris said. Unbeknownst to her, Harris had become an improvisational quilter. "That's the way I work, it just kind of happens. It's all up here," Harris said, pointing to her head.

Harris's quilts have often been compared to jazz music, a metaphor she welcomes. "I see music and rhythm visually," Harris said. "Some of my earlier work

is very rhythmic. Even though it's improvisational, I consciously try to create rhythm." A series of her works, called *Singing, Dancing, and All That Jazz*, includes quilts titled *Blues in the Night, Something like a Jitterbug*, and *Dancing in the Streets*. Harris likens her quilt-making process to the work of her favorite jazz musicians, like Thelonious Monk and Duke Ellington. "It's a variation on a theme. [...] You know the melody, but the fun of it is finding the melody in what they're playing around it."

The colorful and sometimes three-dimensional style of Harris's work has also been influenced by her interest in ethnographic textiles. A self-described entrepreneur, Harris headed an interior design firm for decades. During an economic

downturn, she turned her office into a shop selling art and objects from around the world. "There was a time when I considered getting an anthropology degree because I see a common thread in all the cultures," Harris said. Every nook of her home holds a treasure: textiles from Africa, baskets from Southeast Asia, a sequin Vodou flag from Haiti, and more.

"A lot of my work was influenced by Yoruba textiles," Harris said. The Yoruba people live in parts of Nigeria and Benin and create elaborate and colorful pieced garments for a masquerade ritual called *egungun*. "I was enchanted by the visuals. [The garments] look a lot like a quilt, lots of patchwork." Harris imagined how these garments might look in motion. "Seeing those panels overlapping, swinging, and dancing — it was fascinating." Harris started working in three dimensions, creating more texture in her quilts, and incorporating pieced panels into her work — styles that she has explored throughout her career.

Harris's work is also influenced by her beloved city of Detroit. "You can't help but be influenced by your environment," said Harris. "If I lived in the country, I would probably make trees and rivers and streams, but that's not what I see around me." A lifelong resident of Detroit, Harris said, "I may see a bunch of kids walking, wearing differently colored clothes, bumping up against each other. To me, that's a quilt."

ABOVE: Quilts rich in meaning and created with superb skill all begin with a few scraps and some thread. **OPPOSITE:** Embroidery, reverse appliqué, *sashiko* stitches — many techniques come together in Harris's studio.

Harris will sometimes use the reverse side of a textile, such as this *mola*, to intentionally highlight imperfections.

Detroit beautiful

Cityscapes, a series of Harris's improvisational quilts, reflects her lived environment. Picking up her *Blues in the Night* quilt, Harris said, "It's the skyline, but I didn't set out for it to be." The quilt features Harris's signature use of black solids, piecing that defies a traditional grid, and angled panels reminiscent of the city's sharp lines. "It was a very improvisational piece. I probably thought I'd use these colors, and then the rooftops started to emerge." This quilt, also part of Harris's jazz-inspired series, became a perfect illustration of the artist's improvisational style and desire to evoke the beauty of her city.

"For so long, Detroit has been trashed," Harris said. "People always talk about how bad it is, and it's never been bad for me." Harris said she's had many opportunities to move to other parts of the country, but she's never leaving Detroit. "The biggest asset here is the people. Visitors always say the people are so nice. Why wouldn't I want to live in a place like that? What I have here is so vibrant."

Retirement has opened up the time and space for Harris to explore new techniques and visuals. On a Mediterranean cruise in 2011, she stood in a centuries-old church and noticed peeling paint that covered a beautiful mosaic. She started seeing layers of aging everywhere — city walls where old posters peeled off, ripples in the sand from waves, and more. "These layers tell stories of time and place," Harris said. She saw layers on old buildings in Detroit and other cities she visited. "[They] seemed to tell stories not only of the building, but also of the people who inhabited the building."

CLOCKWISE FROM UPPER LEFT: This decorative tribal textile, called a *suzani*, comes from Central Asia. The word "suzani" derives from the Persian "suzan" which means "needle"; detail, work in progress; pieces and parts in Harris's home studio.

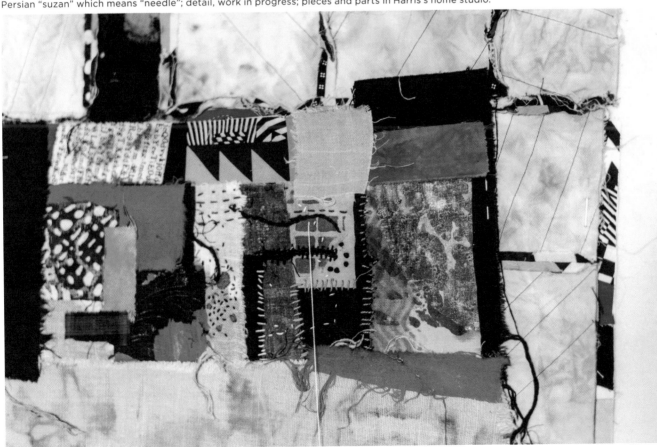

ABOVE: The artist and her husband, writer Bill Harris. **OPPOSITE:** Carole Harris's professional interior design experience and robust art practice mean the Harris home is full of textile treasures.

Time and space

The work Harris has made since retirement is a series called *Mapping Time, Place, and Memory.* Harris is well-known for her geometric piecing and bold colors, but her new explorations have taken her in a completely new direction. Harris now rust-dyes fabric. She rips fabric instead of cutting, because as she said, "I don't think nature gives you perfect edges." She also experiments with reverse appliqué and fusibles. Harris's work is still improvisational, but she said, "This is the first time I've really thought narratively. I think these little areas of texture and overlay are mini-stories."

Harris used words like scratches, scrapes, scars, mending, erosion, and patina to describe her recent work. She said the ideas have been "incubating" for years and thinks her new direction grew out of her *Cityscapes* series and her interest in Japanese *boro.*

These days, Harris's schedule is filled with exhibits of her quilts, including shows at the Detroit Institute of Arts, the University of Michigan, Saginaw Valley State University, and Oakland University this year alone. What's next for Harris after this slew of exhibits? As she said, "There's no shortage of ideas. I'm always ready to try something new."

Harris has loved every phase of her half-century quilting career, but she knows there's something special happening in retirement. Her design firm often dictated how much quilting she could do, with busy times keeping Harris away from her sewing machine. "At this stage in my life, I'm exploring and really coming into my own as a professional artist," Harris said. "It's so rewarding to me and I'm enjoying making more than ever."

BIRD'S NEST BARN QUILTS

When Joanne Dotson built the tiny cabin nestled behind her house, she never dreamed she would start a business making some of the most innovative barn quilts since the barn-quilt movement started in 2001. The charming 15-by-10-foot room is where Dotson now runs her Bird's Nest Barn Quilts workshop.

On a road trip to Kentucky in 2015, Dotson saw a barn quilt for the first time. Not being a quilter, she wasn't sure what it was, but she loved what she saw: a beautifully painted wooden square in bright colors, hanging on the side of a bed-and-breakfast. "I started reading about barn quilts and I just loved it," said Dotson. After experimenting with layering paint on a pressure-treated wood square for her first barn quilt, she developed a system and realized she could help others create painted heirlooms. "I want them to last for generations, just like real quilts."

Dotson's experiments with color and technique have received the seal of approval from Donna Sue Groves, creator of the barn-quilt trend started in 2001 in Ohio. Groves complimented Dotson's barn quilts, particularly her use of decorative stenciling that gives her barn quilts the look of real fabric prints and piecing.

Bird's Nest Barn Quilts has also gotten the seal of approval from happy repeat customers like quilter Laura Overton who has made small barn quilts for each season and brought friends to workshops. Debbie McCormick, a quilter for over 20 years, had tried to make barn quilts without guidance, but her first attempts peeled, cracked, and warped. "I took a class [with Joanne] and saw how professional she is. It made all the difference," McCormick said. She and Dotson have become friends since that first class. Community building is an important aspect of Dotson's six-to-ten hour workshops.

Dotson wants every building in her town of Carleton, Michigan, to sport a barn quilt. "You can put a barn quilt on any building, even something that is worn down," said Dotson. "It just brings out the beauty." And while Dotson loves barn quilts, she doesn't plan to make a real fabric quilt anytime soon. "I could make one, but I love painting them so much. It makes me feel so peaceful and creative. [...] Once I'm doing a barn quilt, it kind of consumes me." With a smile, she asked, "Is that what it's like, making a regular quilt?"

FROM LEFT: School supplies; in the workshop space, textiles bring texture to the walls; a student's Log Cabin "block" hangs proudly on the front porch.

BY **Laura McDowell Hopper**

Lizzy House
A GARDEN OF POSSIBILITIES

———————

Lizzy House donned her favorite wide-brimmed hat and turned on her car. A rendition of "My Funny Valentine" by jazz pianist Erroll Garner played softly on the radio. We were on our way from the thirty-something's cozy Ann Arbor apartment to her spacious plot in a local community garden to catch up on her life and work since leaving the quilt industry.

After a decade of designing quilts and fabric, House no longer quilts. Today, she grows bee-friendly plants in her garden, makes collaborative ceramics with her husband, and sells essential oils through her business, The Bee Squad. She also creates beautiful *pajaki* — symbolic Polish objects, made of paper, that resemble chandeliers. Quilts, gardening, ceramics, and her business have all helped House through dark times in her life. We may know Lizzy House's whimsical fabric and cheerful quilt designs, but getting to know the former quilt designer herself is an experience rife with surprises.

All the world's her studio: Lizzy House in Ann Arbor.

For fabric lovers, House's cheerful, graphic prints are irresistible; few modern-style quilters don't have at least a fat quarter or two of her ubiquitous "Pearl Bracelet" print in their stash.

The kid is alright

Most children aspire to jobs like doctor, lawyer, or police officer. But not all children. "I decided when I was six that I would design fabric," House said. In the 1980s and 1990s, her mother, Cherri House, made her clothes but the prints didn't speak to Lizzy's sensibilities until one day, she found a fabric she loved. "It was an off-white fabric with dusty blue bows," she said. House asked her mother how the fabric came to exist — and right then and there, a fabric designer was born.

Years passed and House remained devoted to her career aspirations. In seventh grade, she tried to make her dream a reality. "I called a fabric manufacturer and asked if they were taking submissions from new designers," she said with a laugh. "These were all words that my mother was feeding to me because a seventh grader doesn't know how to ask [these things]."

To House's surprise, the manufacturer was accepting submissions and asked if her collection was floral or geometric. "I covered up the phone and whispered to my mom, 'Is it floral or geometric?' She said, 'It's geometric,' and they said, 'Great, send us all your stuff.'" The experience was a wake-up call to the young House who realized she needed to work harder: She began practicing her designs in Microsoft Paint.

In a serendipitous turn of events, House played Lucy in a 2006 college production of *You're a Good Man, Charlie Brown* where Snoopy was played by Katie Brandeburg, daughter of quilt pattern designer Barbara Brandeburg of Cabbage Rose. At a cast dinner, House told Brandeburg about her fabric design dreams and Brandeburg encouraged her. This early affirmation from somebody on the inside bolstered House. "It feels so ominous when you're on the outside, like a bubble you can't pop," she said.

After a trip to Belgium that same year, House returned home to tragic news. "My cat of 14 years was killed in our front yard," House said with tears

in her eyes. "I didn't know what to do with myself. [...] I felt this impression that quilting would help." Although House was interested in fabric design, she had never made a quilt before. "That was the first quilt that I made. [...] I put all of my love for her, all of my hurt, and all of the words that I didn't have into making this thing. I've devoted so much of my life to teaching and sharing [quilting] to enable other people to have that kind of healing."

Making this cathartic quilt after the death of her beloved pet motivated House to become part of the quilt industry. She designed a vibrant fabric line inspired by one of her great passions — cooking — and brought it to Quilt Market. Nearly every fabric company said no to her fabric designs, but Andover Fabrics gave her a yes. At age 21, House saw her first collection burst onto the quilt scene and change the visual landscape of modern fabric design.

In the decade House worked in the quilt industry, she released 10 patterns, designed 18 fabric collections, and went on a 50-city tour teaching quilters to make her *Meadow* quilt. "Teaching people to make *Meadow* became so much more about the oral tradition of quilting, the historic sharing of why we quilt, and passing on this knowledge as opposed to me selling a paper pattern," said House. This experience helped her see how quilting could follow different models than what the industry sometimes dictates.

"In the beginning, [designing fabric] was exciting and it was what I wanted to do," House said. "I definitely have gone my own way in the industry, [...] but I decided somewhere along the way that I didn't want to monetize quilting." Feeling that demands for her fabric restricted her growth as an artist, House made a clean break from working in the quilt industry and started exploring new mediums and healing practices. "I decided I was going to do the things I've always wanted to do but had no time for because I was on somebody else's timeline."

ABOVE, OPPOSITE: House's 2015 quilt, *Life Cycles,* expands the rainbow. Quilting by Jo Thomas.

Whether she's working in flowers or fabric, House finds the color.

A new healing journey

Red squirrels danced through the plants and grasshoppers chirped as the sun started to set. House walked the rows of her garden plot pointing to zinnias, eggplants, beans, squash, tomatoes, and sunflowers. She said hello to native bees flying through the purple borage. "I started gardening in 2012," House said. "As soon as I did, I realized this is part of who I am."

House's connection to plants and animals shines through her fabric designs: Whimsical cats, flowers, unicorns, and butterflies are sprinkled throughout her prints. But while she was designing these fabrics, House struggled to work. Along with suffering from depression, she went through what she calls a "complete life upheaval" of getting married, moving across the country, and contemplating a career change. She turned to nature for help with her overwork and stress and tried essential oils.

"I didn't know anything about oils other than that I was hurting and I was willing to try," she said. "I used this oil and in minutes I found relief that nothing else had given me."

At first, House never dreamed she could make a radical move from a successful quilt career to her newfound passion for natural healing. But she's glad she made the change, and she continues to connect with quilters in her new role. "Many of my customers are quilters looking for help," said House. "So much of what I'm doing now and what I've been called to do on this planet is help people heal. Mostly it's been through my artwork, but [now] I see that it's more."

House has traded in designing fabric for designing original pamphlets, packaging, and enamel pins for her business. "I will always find a surface and beautify it," she said with a smile.

CLOCKWISE FROM UPPER LEFT: Cabbage in bloom; a label-to-be on the back of *Life Cycles*; a girl and her garden.

ABOVE: Inspiration and art, including a sketch of one of her famous cat designs, cover the walls. **OPPOSITE:** House's journey through the quilt industry had its challenges, but she cherishes the connections she made when teaching workshops.

ABOVE: Lizzy at home. OPPOSITE: The garden is the perfect place for a dazzling *pajak* made by House.

> *"I do feel like textiles will always be a part of my life in a very real and tangible way."*
>
> — LIZZY HOUSE

Pajaki *and roller skates*

Hanging one of her *pajaki* in her garden, House explained more about the Polish tradition. "There's a lot of ethnography with it just like with quilting," she said. "[*Pajaki*] are made in the darkest time of the year, with things people collect all year to get them through to the lightest time of the year. They [represent] a celebration of light." House has made *pajaki* out of leftover invitations from her wedding, treasured Liberty of London paper, and other small objects that bring her joy. In Poland, she explained, "traditionally at the end of the summer solstice, they burn [these] in preparation for the next year." *Pajaki* are made to be temporary.

Most quilts are made to be permanent. They are treasured family heirlooms, passed down from generation to generation, and sometimes even pre-

served in museums. Snuggling into a quilt can help anyone heal, but the process of making quilts can also help us through dark times.

Some folks are inspired to make quilts for the rest of their lives. Others stop quilting or take a break when their healing journey evolves. The life cycle we go through as quilters is unique to each of us. Even though she's not making quilts now, House said, "I do feel like textiles will always be a part of my life in a very real and tangible way."

House is always on the lookout for something new and challenging. When asked what adventure she plans next, she replied, "I'm going to get kick-ass at roller-skating." In textiles or on wheels, Lizzie House continues to be full of surprises — and we can't wait to see what's next.

MID MICHIGAN

Beauty from Edge to Edge

MID MICHIGAN

TO MAKE THE MOST of *Quiltfolk* location trips, our path through a given state may be dictated by maps and efficiency, rather than by specific attractions — and yet this path often reveals myriad surprises. We knew there was a lot to see in Central Michigan, but as we made our way across the "middle part," we captured stories we might have missed, had we simply taken a different route.

In this part of the world, there are factories in cities like Grand Rapids and Lansing and small farms everywhere in between; there are a dozen universities and too many cherry stands to count. Our lateral path across Michigan's center resulted in stories and visuals that capture the wide variety of experiences across the region — and we're about to take you on that same journey of discovery. We found patchwork and quilt-themed murals in unexpected places. At MSU, one of the biggest universities in the nation, we saw one of the most prized quilt collections in the world. We met budding quilters — and chased chickens — on a farm. And we're thrilled to bring you a very special series of photographs featuring the work of Mary Schafer, a legendary quilt figure from centrally located Flint.

The path we took across the center of Michigan was so rich in stories and quilts, this section of the magazine planned itself. Thanks, Michigan!

BY **Laura McDowell Hopper**

Teacher, Teacher
LYNN CARSON HARRIS

Kids spend a lot of time in front of screens, but not at Lynn Carson Harris's after-school sewing club. Carson Harris has taught young people how to quilt for over 20 years and currently runs a sewing club at her studio in the small town of Chelsea, Michigan. She also runs a beginner's summer sewing camp in her home. On her property in idyllic Washtenaw County, chickens roam freely, a swing hangs in the center of her barn, and there's an in-ground trampoline for kids to "get out their wiggles," as Carson Harris says.

We met four of Carson Harris's most dedicated middle-school-aged quilters – Phoebe (Carson Harris's daughter), Ottilia, Catie, and Zoe – at the barn where they had all taken their shoes off to jump on the trampoline together. The girls talked to us about their favorite classes at school, what they want to be when they grow up, and why they love improv quilting. After getting to know the girls in the sewing club, it was easy to see why Carson Harris says teaching them is the best part of her job.

School's in for the summer. Four of Lynn Carson Harris's students, from left: Phoebe, Catie, Zoe, and Ottilia.

ABOVE: In large pieces or small, Carson Harris works in vibrant, saturated color. OPPOSITE: Ottilia, 13, knows her way around a sewing machine (and a quilt shop).

An early start

When Carson Harris was a child, her mother taught children's sewing classes. As Carson Harris grew up and made her career in quilting, spending time sewing with kids seemed like a natural path for her to follow. "It's the best afternoon time I could ask for," she said. "They're not gossiping or talking about new fabric lines. They come in excited and say 'Oh my gosh, I just finished this book, you guys should all read it.'"

Carson Harris was a quilter who always followed directions until she met legendary Michigan quilter Gwen Marston. "It was a life-changing experience for me," Carson Harris said. "I had never done quilting without knowing what I was going to end up with."

She struggled the first time Marston taught her to make a wonky Liberated Star block. But after a few tries, Carson Harris made a Liberated Star she liked and fell in love with a freer, more improvisational style of quilting. She has attended Marston's Beaver Island retreat nearly every year and the two have become close friends.

Now Carson Harris teaches the improvisational patchwork techniques she learned from Marston to children in her club. "Nothing seems overwhelming or hard to them," said Carson Harris. "Sometimes the adult quilters [to whom] I teach improvisational piecing struggle, but the kids are willing to try something new."

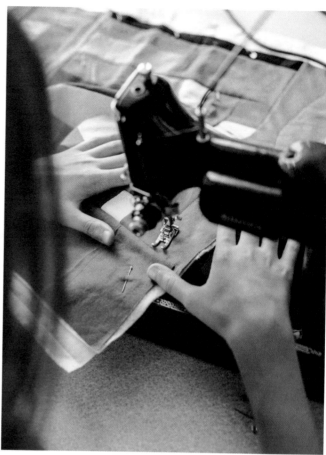

ABOVE: Creativity in progress. **BELOW:** Catie and Carson Harris's daughter, Phoebe, enjoying their sewing time before an ice cream break.

Zoe's quilt patches are simply charming.

And the girls take well to this approach. Phoebe and Ottilia are working on an improv collaboration. They each made panels they had planned to turn into tote bags, but instead of making their own bags, they decided to combine their panels to create one bag. Both girls picked shades of blue, but Ottilia's panel has a scrappy mix of prints and Phoebe's features solids she picked to look like the ocean. When they finish making their tote bag, the girls feel it will be the perfect combination of their personalities.

Zoe, the youngest member of the club, also fell in love with improv. "It's a lot more free and you get to have more fun with it than quilting with a pattern," she said. "You make more decisions on it because with improv quilting, if you mess up, you can just make it into something else."

Old School Sewing, Carson Harris's studio where the club meets, is equipped with a fleet of Featherweight sewing machines. Over the years, Carson Harris has learned that Featherweights are great for teaching kids to sew. "There are less distractions on a Featherweight. They're smaller, they're cute, and there's not much that goes wrong," she said. Carson Harris also noted that many of her students sew at home with their grandmothers. Using Featherweights in her studio means the kids are more familiar with the vintage machines their grandmothers use.

ABOVE: Quilter Gwen Marston gave Carson Harris this small quilt, which now hangs in the classroom space.
OPPOSITE: Teacher, friend, mother, entrepreneur, artist — Lynn Carson Harris has plenty of experience worth sharing.

Looking to the next generation

Most of the girls in Carson Harris's club love sewing at home, except for Catie who says her two younger brothers blaze a noisy path of destruction through her house. Catie is outgoing but quiet, and peaceful spaces like the sewing studio are important to her, just as they are to many adult quilters. After learning to sew from her grandmother, she made four quilts and plans to make many more. Catie's search for quiet spaces often takes her to the library. "Librarians are my superheroes," she said.

Phoebe, who has already been sewing for about a decade, loves sewing at home with Carson Harris. "My mom started teaching me to quilt on paper when I was still in preschool," she said, describing Carson Harris's method for introducing kids to the feel of a sewing machine without unruly fabric. Last year, Phoebe made a fabric banner for her math teacher with all the digits of Pi she had memorized (it used to be 122 digits). Lately she balances sewing with watching the *Great British Sewing Bee*, reading, and playing her cello. She hopes to get a cello scholarship to pay for college when she's older.

Ottilia also sews at home and got a new sewing machine for Christmas. She's been making small projects, like pouches. What does Ottilia want to do when she grows up? "First, I'm going to survive high school," she said with a laugh. Ottilia has been in theater productions of *Shrek The Musical*, *It's a Wonderful Life*, and *Alice in Wonderland*. She hopes to go to a performing arts college. "Ottilia, when

ABOVE: The future of quilting is bright. **OPPOSITE:** Sixth-grader Zoe is already at work on her next quilt, a Log Cabin.

you're a famous actor, will you fund my library?" Catie asked. Ottilia thought to herself for a moment and said, "Sure!"

Zoe's grandmother taught her to quilt and Zoe loves it so much that she is the only girl who goes to the sewing club twice a week. As the youngest in the group, Zoe has plenty of time to figure out what she wants to do when she grows up, but she already has big plans like her friend Ottilia. "I want to go to Julliard and be an actor," she said. She's already landed stage roles as Snow White in *Snow White* and Wendy in *Peter Pan*, and she wants to take choir classes.

Each of the girls in the after-school club at Old School Sewing have sewing ambitions. For now, Zoe is working on a Log Cabin quilt made with koala fabric; Phoebe and Ottilia are almost done with

their tote-bag collaboration; and Catie is working on her fifth quilt. During *Quiltfolk*'s visit to the sewing studio, the kids worked and complimented each other's projects. They talked about classes and school plays and, from time to time, Carson Harris stepped in to give the kids tips on cutting fabric, choosing color, and quilting.

The girls spent an hour sewing for the pure joy of it, none of them worried about perfect points or designer fabrics. "They're at the perfect age," Carson Harris said. "They don't stress about sewing. It's a hobby and they're treating it like [one]. It's fun for them." And as our time with the girls came to a close over a round of ice cream cones, we reflected on the freedom inherent in simple, unadulterated creativity. We could all learn lessons from these budding quilters' easy-going approach to the craft.

BY **Mary Fons**

Sweet as Candy
DOLL QUILTS BY MARY SCHAFER

To scratch the surface of quilt history and culture in Michigan is to discover the exuberant life and times of Mary Schafer (1910-2007).

A prolific quilter and natural quilt historian, Schafer has been credited with keeping quiltmaking and quilt scholarship alive during the mid-20th century fallow period. After World War II and before the revival began in the 1970s, quiltmaking experienced a kind of recession due to changing fashions and cultural forces that devalued the quilt — but not for Schafer. By keeping records, collecting, and sharing everything she learned with everyone who would listen, Schafer kept the home fires burning for quilters in America, even if they wouldn't appreciate it until later.

One of Schafer's biggest fans and best friends was fellow Michigander Gwen Marston, who spent 30 years visiting Schafer and her husband Fred outside Flint and soaking up history and technique from the exceptional quilter. Schafer made mostly bed-size quilts, but in 1982, after reading Thomas K. Woodard and Blanche Greenstein's *Crib Quilts and Other Small Wonders* (1981), both she and Marston fell in love with making doll quilts. Schafer said whipping up one of these smaller quilts was "like eating candy."

Perhaps Schafer, who was born in Austria-Hungary just before World War I and who spent a year in an American orphanage as a young girl after the death of her mother, found a certain solace in making dozens upon dozens of these small quilts; she gifted many of them to Marston. Or perhaps the spirited, warm Mary Schafer loved making these quilts simply because, like her beloved Michigan, they were beautiful.

The following photo essay was made possible by Gwen Marston, who graciously allowed *Quiltfolk* to photograph her collection of Mary Schafer doll quilts. Each quilt was a gift to Marston from Schafer herself. All quilts photographed on Beaver Island.

BY **Meg Cox**

Pat Holly & Sue Nickels
THE TWO OF US

Winners of top prizes at the big AQS show in Paducah every year are given canvas director's chairs emblazoned with their names. Over the years, sisters Sue Nickels and Pat Holly have won nine of these "champ chairs" between them, enough to host a dinner party.

They'd have to decide which of their houses in Ann Arbor, Michigan, should be the venue for dinner, but you can bet that Nickels and Holly would not fight about it: These two leading ladies on the national quilt stage work as a tight team, whether teaching classes together or co-creating those prize-winning quilts.

"We played well together as little girls and we still do," said Nickels. Today at ages 64 and 65, they are famous for making dazzling collaborative quilts like *The Beatles Quilt* and *The Space Quilt* now owned by The National Quilt Museum.

Two quilt-world rock stars are better than one. Pat Holly (L) and Sue Nickels (R) in Ann Arbor.

Blue Garden

hand pieced by Leatha (Tiny) Holly
machine quilted by Pat Holly

started 1990's
finished 9-1-2010
Ann Arbor, Michigan

CLOCKWISE FROM UPPER LEFT: Quilts and fabric warm the Holly home; in 2010, Holly finished *Blue Garden*, started in 1990 by their mother Leatha, affectionately known as "Tiny"; Pat Holly takes her time.

Discussing the fine art of fine quilting in Pat Holly's second-floor studio.

The sisters are also well-known for their close association with fellow Michigander Gwen Marston. After Nickels and Holly attended almost every year of Marston's famous quilt retreat, the founder handed over the reins to the sisters. The Holly Girls Quilt Retreats (Holly is their maiden name, which Pat kept when she married) run for four weeks in a row each fall at the White Birch Lodge in Elk Rapids. Like Marston's, each year's camp focuses on a theme: In 2018, it was the Trip Around the World pattern.

Dressed casually in black slacks and knit tops, the sisters demonstrated their practical, easy teamwork as they welcomed the *Quiltfolk* crew into Holly's gracious suburban brick home. "We chose Pat's house to start because hers is bigger," said Nickels.

Together they have sorted and arranged neat piles of quilts in Holly's upstairs studio to showcase the arc of their quilting history, separately and together.

Although Holly and Nickels share Marston's deep love of antique quilts and still call them a chief source of inspiration, the sisters are famed for their skills at machine-appliqué and machine-quilting.

Both took up quilting back in the late 1970s and early 1980s when anyone who didn't piece and quilt by hand was considered a cheat. Nickels recalls that it took her years to complete the first quilt she made that got accepted into a show, in 1988, because the intricately pieced sampler quilt was completely handsewn. "I named the quilt *Wishful Thinking* because I kept wishing for it to be finished," she said.

ABOVE: Detail, *Tea at Tenby* (2008). On the preceding page, the sisters hold up the full *Tea at Tenby* quilt, a collaboration inspired by the pair's annual trips to England. **OPPOSITE:** Illustrating the sisters' relentless attention to detail, *All You Need Is Love* is a smaller version of their world-famous *The Beatles Quilt*.

About that time, the two discovered Harriet Hargrave, a pioneer teacher who proved that the term "heirloom machine-quilting" (the title of her 1985 groundbreaking book) was not an oxymoron. Those skills were added to their own creative training: Both women had attended art school, although Holly began her career as a scientist running an electron microscope lab in a hospital.

Before long, Holly and Nickels became machine-quilting gurus in their own right, catapulted into the limelight with their 1998 Best-of-Show award in Paducah for their vibrant, playful *Beatles* quilt. It wowed with a palette of lime green, pinks, and blues borrowed from the cover of the *Sgt. Pepper's Lonely Hearts Club Band* album cover and featured such familiar images as a yellow submarine rendered in a folk-art style. The sisters had made quilts together before, but this project — dreamed up while they watched a TV documentary about the rock group — made them quilt-world celebrities.

A few years later, the pair decided to co-create *The Space Quilt*, an appliqué masterpiece featuring NASA-inspired imagery. Their father was a test pilot and engineer who was passionate about the space program and watched every launch with his young daughters. *The Space Quilt* won the Machine Workmanship Award in Paducah in 2004 and a top machine-quilting award at Quilt Festival in Houston in 2003.

Amazingly, these two quilts and other joint projects were made during a 20-year stretch when the sisters lived three hours apart. Nickels has lived in the same house in Ann Arbor for 40 years, but Holly moved her family as her husband's job changed. When she and her family lived in Muskegon, on the shore of Lake Michigan, she and Nickels would arrange to meet in the middle, Lansing, to strategize and share their progress.

ABOVE, FROM LEFT: Nickels and Holly, respectively, rely on each other in art and life; at right, Holly holds a mini-quilt made from a design in her 2016 coloring book, *A Miniature World*. **OPPOSITE:** Detail, *Blackbirds Fly* (1996). Inspired by an antique folk-style quilt, this Nickels-and-Holly collaboration features machine-piecing, -quilting, and -appliqué.

Roots and branches

As is typical of their collaborations, they never seem to argue about who does what: "I was mainly the quilter on our collaborations and Pat was mainly the piecer," Nickels explained. "We both love appliqué, so we divide that up."

In the decade since Holly moved back to Ann Arbor, the sisters have spent lots of time together. Nickels is on the road frequently, teaching at shows and guilds and on cruises; Holly is more of a homebody. But Holly makes good use of her time: her meticulous silk appliqué quilts, often influenced by foreign travel, keep winning solo awards for her. She won the award for Best Miniature at the Paducah AQS quilt show four times.

Clearly, both women highly value craftsmanship and spend concentrated time making their masterpieces. Nickels once estimated she spends up to 100 hours quilting a single quilt, and she has spent up to 10 hours doing the appliqué work on a single block.

It may be hard for an outsider to tell who did what block in a shared work, but the sisters do have their differences in methods: "I always say that in the design sense, my machine quilting is more voluptuous and Pat's quilts are more tight and tiny," explained Nickels. "I'm a little more loosey-goosey. You could figure out that she's the organized one just by looking at our sock drawers: Pat's is organized by color and very neat, and my socks are just thrown in there."

These joined creative souls, who inked the lyrics to every Beatles song on the back of their tribute quilt to the Fab Four, bring to mind their poignant 1969 song "The Two of Us": *"You and I have memories / Longer than the road that stretches out ahead / [...] We're on our way home / We're going home."* 🄀

BY **Laura McDowell Hopper**

Dream Team

QUILT HISTORY
ALL-STARS AT MSU

———————

In the early 1970s, hard at work on her master's degree, Dr. Marsha MacDowell took an American art history course. "I proposed to write about my family's quilts, and the professor said that was an inappropriate subject," MacDowell said, in a voice suggesting she still can't believe the misguided comment. "I think that actually lit the fire under me to realize I cannot have a man tell me that this artistic expression is not important."

Since then, MacDowell has co-authored over 60 books and articles on quilt studies, co-curated 25 quilt exhibits, and built a collection of over 1,000 quilts from around the world. As curator of Folk Arts, she has also built a dream team of quilt scholars at the Michigan State University (MSU) Museum — Mary Worrall, Lynne Swanson, and Beth Donaldson — who have worked collaboratively for decades to uncover some of the most understudied topics in quilt history.

FROM LEFT: Marsha MacDowell, Mary Worrall, Beth Donaldson, and Lynne Swanson are better together on the campus of Michigan State University.

ABOVE: MacDowell holds her great-grandmother's scrapbook. OPPOSITE: This Redwork quilt (ca. 1950) was made by MacDowell's great-grandmother, Metta Rybolt, with embroidery help from MacDowell's mother, Betty MacDowell.

A quilter in every family

"I've had a collection of quilts ever since I was born," MacDowell said, showing us a Redwork quilt under which she slept as a child. MacDowell's cherished personal quilt collection includes a quilt made by family as a gift for her graduation; one with photo transfers of her family; and a signature quilt that belonged to her great-grandmother.

The most precious object in MacDowell's personal collection is a scrapbook made by her great-grandmother Nona Alice Ginger Lane. A Detroit quilter, Lane filled her green scrapbook with clippings from a Depression-era *Detroit News* column called "Quilt Club Corner." A clipping about an Indigenous quilter in Lane's scrapbook launched MacDowell's inquiry of Native American quilts that

led to the 1997 landmark book *To Honor and Comfort: Native Quilting Traditions*. "I think it was all seeded here," MacDowell said of her research connection to her great-grandmother.

Although MacDowell's career has centered on quilt studies, she has only made one quilt in her life, piecing together blocks made by family members with help from her coworkers. "The setting of the blocks was designed by Beth [Donaldson] and she oversaw every step of me piecing together the blocks," she said.

Donaldson, on the other hand, has designed and made quilts for decades. Before beginning her job as the quilt collections assistant and coordinator of the Quilt Index *(see page 166)*, Donaldson, a woman as

CLOCKWISE FROM UPPER LEFT: Donaldson, with the quilt she says is "a real conversation starter"; detail, *No, But It's My Dog*; Worrall used a rainbow of batiks in this quilt she gave to her husband for Christmas years ago.

Swanson, an MSU grad herself, shows a Trip Around the World from her personal collection.

funny as she is warm, worked at an East Lansing quilt shop for years. Donaldson's beloved former pet, Mickey the Love Dog, is the subject of a quilt she made in 2004. "This quilt is called *No, But It's My Dog*, because everybody looks at it and asks, 'Is that your house?' and I say, 'No, but it's my dog!'"

Like Donaldson, Curator of Cultural Heritage Mary Worrall worked at a local quilt shop in the early days of her museum career. Her paycheck went back into fabrics she purchased there, including those used to make a Star quilt for the first Christmas she spent with her husband. "I guess it's a sign that if I wanted to put all this time into a quilt, our relationship was really going somewhere," Worrall said with a smile.

Worrall also considers her coworkers part of her family. "Part of our story here is how important a work family can be," Worrall said. In her hands, she held two quilts made for her children by Donaldson, Swanson, and colleague Pearl Yee Wong. "I work with this tiny group of women who are so awesome and meaningful and such a big part of my life. You can see that in the quilts they made for my kids."

Lynne Swanson, collections manager and assistant curator of Folk Arts, made her first quilt in 2014 when her son left for college. "These ladies finally convinced me to make a quilt," Swanson said with a laugh. She is a new quilter, but Swanson has been working at the MSU Museum since graduate school. In 1985, she joined the museum's Michigan Quilt Project team that documented over 10,000 quilts and published the book *Michigan Quilts: 150 Years of a Textile Tradition* (MacDowell and Fitzgerald, Eds., 1987).

ABOVE: Landon Hall, named for the university's first female professor, on MSU's manicured campus. **OPPOSITE:** One of Lynne Swanson's favorite quilts inside the collection, Stuart Ansell's quilted homage to the Detroit Tigers.

The MSU Museum holds a collection of nearly one million cultural, historic, and natural-history objects, but the 1,000-piece quilt collection is the jewel of the museum's holdings; caring for it is the best part of Swanson's job. She loves the personal and historic connections that quilts create. In the museum's state-of-the-art collections storage, Swanson showed the *Quiltfolk* team a recently acquired quilt.

"This is an amazing, iconic piece of Michigan sports history," Swanson said. The quilt, made by Detroit police officer Stuart Ansell in the 1930s, celebrates the 1934 American League pennant-winning Detroit Tigers team. Ansell gathered autographs from each member of the winning team

and embroidered them onto the quilt. Swanson said this quilt reminds her of her grandmother. "My Grandma Hansen was born in 1890 and loved the Tigers since the beginning of the team's existence in 1894," she said.

The people who care for quilts at the MSU Museum have strong personal ties to quilts, but they are also quick to point out the academic value of their remarkable collection. "The Tigers quilt helps us open doors to teach students about Depression-era Detroit," said Worrall. "Sometimes with fun objects like this, we can get students talking in a different way than in traditional classroom settings."

Scandalous Sue

Asking the quilt team to choose their favorite piece in the museum's collection is impossible. The collection has works from quilt superstars Mary Schafer, Cuesta Benberry, and Carolyn L. Mazloomi. The staff also cares for Native American, Hawaiian, South African, Chinese, and Southeast Asian quilts. There are historic quilts and contemporary quilts, pattern quilts and social-justice-themed quilts. With a collection this large and impressive, how could they pick a single favorite? But there's one spectacular quilt that, as Donaldson said, "we all love."

Made in 1979 by a group of quilters called the Seamsters Union Local #500, the infamous *The Sun Sets on Sunbonnet Sue* features 20 blocks that show ways in which the popular appliqué motif Sunbonnet Sue might die — for example, suicide by hanging or consumption by snake. The quilt caused an immediate controversy, with one show organizer saying, "A lot of gruesome types of happenings take place in our lifetimes [...] but that doesn't mean they should be commemorated in a quilt. That type of humor is sick."

Today, this controversial quilt has an important place in the museum's prestigious collection. Worrall, who remembers when she first saw the quilt in a textbook called *The Power of Feminist Art* (Broude and Garrard, Eds., 1996), uses this quilt to teach students. "This is such a nice entry for students because it is cartoonish, it shows pop culture, and it's not what they expect," Worrall said, adding that many of the blocks — like her favorite, showing Skylab falling on Sunbonnet Sue — are "prehistory" for today's students.

Quilt historian Barbara Brackman, who designed and made two of the blocks in the controversial quilt, is happy *Sue* still has much to say. "We certainly had no idea the quilt would have such long legs (actually, Sue has no legs). There is a lot written about it saying we were protesting [about] women's rights and positions in society. But as artists, we were mostly upset by crimes against aesthetics and literally wanted to kill her off. Sentimentality and cuteness were anathema."

The MSU Museum collection has a special focus on unexpected and under-researched quilts. Their exhibit and award-winning book *Quilts and Human Rights* focused on social justice quilts, like one of Worrall's favorite pieces. Titled *Ruby Bridges: What a Difference a School Makes*, the quilt by Marion Coleman opens up conversations about segregation. "I'm interested in the power of objects and the use of quilts to connect with students," said Worrall. "So many people connect with quilts. They're a really great starting point to talk about social issues."

Worrall and the rest of the team are meticulous in research and preservation; on the table, the controversial *Sun Sets on Sunbonnet Sue* quilt.

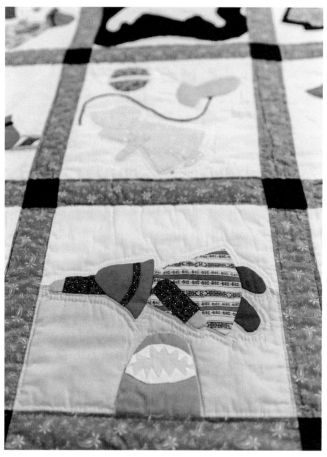

v School   New Orleans, Louisiana   November 1960

Brown v. Board of Education
May 17, 1954

ABOVE: Detail, *Ruby Bridges: What a Difference a School Makes* by Marion Coleman (2006). When Mary Worrall was asked to name a favorite piece in the collection, she chose Coleman's powerful quilt. **OPPOSITE:** In addition to quilts, the museum collects ephemera, records, and items such as these loose patchwork pieces made in Mississippi in the mid-19th century. Each object broadens the collection's scope.

ABOVE: One of many quilts shared with us inside the collections room was an 1873 Baltimore Album featuring an early "quilt-as-you-go" technique. **OPPOSITE:** The dream team, standing with a poster for their 1987 book, *Michigan Quilts: 150 Years of a Textile Tradition.* For more about the quilt on the poster, see the AQSG Trunk Show on page 172.

Quilts go off campus

The MSU Museum collection isn't just for students. The team shares the museum's quilts with the world through their publications focused on filling gaps in quilt scholarship, including *Quilts and Health, African American Quiltmaking in Michigan,* and *Quilts of Southwest China.* They also curate nationwide exhibits, manage the Quilt Index, and offer occasional behind-the-scenes quilt viewings for the general public.

Donaldson loves leading behind-the-scenes tours. One of her favorite quilts in the collection, dated 1873, is an early example of machine-quilting as you go. "Everybody thinks that they've found a new technique," Donaldson said jokingly. "They think, 'Nobody's ever done this. I've got to copyright it.'" Donaldson, who has written a quilt pattern book, said she understands that impulse. But she also wants more people to value the long history of quilting. "Somebody's always done a technique before you," she said. It's a lesson she's learned from spending years studying and cataloging

historic quilts at the MSU Museum.

Over the years, the MSU Museum has become known as a place that does quilt research that others don't. "We just kept seeing [these] holes in the quilt scholarship," MacDowell said. "The Michigan Quilt Project in the 1980s put us in contact with all kinds of people." The team continues to ask questions that other scholars do not, and they're currently doing significant research on quilts related to health and quilting in South Africa.

But there's something even more special about this team: their eagerness to collaborate. "One of the things that make us a great team is that we're all interested in different things," Donaldson said. "Marsha is all about the story. Mary loves human rights and contemporary quilts. Lynne is very visual and likes modern quilts. I love old quilts and learning about techniques." Each member of the team at the Michigan State University Museum quilt collection brings a different perspective to their work, and together they have sewn a place in quilt history. ◖

mpp 86.1/31.4

BY Jennifer Ackerman-Haywood

The Quilt Index

If you're one of those people who can't stop clicking on intoxicating quilt photos posted online, you're going to love this: A group of hardworking curators and programmers at MSU has just completed an impressive upgrade of their one-of-a-kind Quilt Index — a vast repository of quilt photos and history.

The highly clickable index (www.quiltindex.org) was created and is currently maintained by faculty and staff at the MSU Museum in East Lansing, Michigan. The index, which documents 90,000 quilts from around the globe, includes quilts from public and private collections, as well as historic textiles from more than 250 museums.

In recent years, this comprehensive quilt database was challenging to navigate and had started to look a bit dated, so its creators decided to update the site and link the data to make it more intuitive and visually stimulating. The upgrade, scheduled to launch in October 2018, has resulted in a more clickable collection featuring enhanced search capabilities and high quality photos that might have an addictive Pinterest effect on quilt enthusiasts.

In addition to showcasing thousands of quilt photos, the index, which officially launched in 2003, provides a plethora of supporting materials including newspaper articles, essays, photos of quilters, ephemera, and lesson plans for teachers. Among the most notable improvements to the site is the increased use of large photos and streamlined searches. The beauty of the index is that it allows access to data that would be very difficult for individuals to track down on their own.

While no one at MSU works full-time on the Quilt Index, Beth Donaldson, a quilt collections assistant and the unofficial chief "data cleaner" behind the index upgrade, has clocked countless hours entering quilt data since MSU began creating the database with grant funding in 1999.

"It's a way to honor the literally thousands of women that went out and documented quilts [...] all over the country, and they weren't being paid," Donaldson said. "They would get the church basement. They would set up the tables. They would set up the frames and they would photograph quilts and write down all the information."

During Michigan's first statewide quilt documentation effort in 1984, the museum staff worked with local organizations "to organize Documentation Days in their communities that were open to all quilts regardless of the quilt's age, technique, or original provenance, as long as there was some sort of Michigan connection," said Mary Worrall, a curator at the museum. While the MSU Museum staff started collecting and cataloging quilt data from their home state, the index later expanded to include quilts and related artifacts from all over the globe when it became clear that no one was curating this valuable quilt history.

Many historic documents detailing quilts and their makers are included in the index, but there is still a lot of data out there that was collected and not entered into the database. "We know where a lot of it is," Donaldson said. "It's a matter of getting access to it, because most of the groups deposited that information in archives in libraries and museums." And once the data goes into an archive, getting access to the original documents can be challenging. "We have collection partners," Worrall said, explaining that the museum does not have the funds to fly curators around the country to collect documents and relies instead on grants, donor support, and volunteers gathering quilt data in their home states.

Detail, quilts in the Cuesta Benberry collection kept at MSU. These quilts, along with tens of thousands of other objects, are painstakingly recorded in the mighty Quilt Index.

When the index launched, the main objective was to preserve and share quilt data from across the country. The new and improved data platform will go beyond this. "We have visually weighted things differently," said Dr. Marsha MacDowell, MSU professor, museum curator, and director of the Quilt Index. "The story is as much about the object as it is about the story of how it was made and the story of the maker."

The museum is adding legacy pages to the index as a way to pay tribute to and memorialize quilters while documenting their lifetime achievements. The first quilter to be featured by the Quilt Legacy Project is Claire Vlasin (1932-2012), an East Lansing quilter and quilt collector who spent much of her adult life making, collecting, and sharing her quilting knowledge.

Vlasin made and gifted many quilts during her life and amassed a large quilt collection that was dispersed after her death. While many of Vlasin's quilts are not accessible to the public at the museums and private collections to which they were donated, "they're all accessible in the Quilt Index," MacDowell said. These quilts, along with a biography submitted by Vlasin's family, can be viewed on the index by searching her name.

In 2019, the MSU Museum plans to launch a new feature that would allow individual quilters to pay a small fee and upload their own quilt photos and documentation to the site. This would allow the database to continue to grow with public support. In the meantime, quilters can commit to labeling and documenting their handmade and collected quilts to prepare to add them to the index. "The beauty is [...] once you get your quilts in there and your story in there, your quilts will be searchable with all the rest of the data," MacDowell said. "We're excited about it."

QUILT INDEX TIMELINE

1981

The Kentucky Quilt Project is launched and credited as the first statewide quilt documentation effort. In a national grassroots effort to document quilts and their makers, many other states soon follow suit, holding Quilt Discovery Days where anyone can bring in a quilt to be recorded.

1984

The MSU Museum launches the Michigan Quilt Project for the purpose of documenting quilts in the state.

1986

A series of African American Community Quilt Discovery Days are held in an effort to document populations underrepresented in the first wave of Documentation Days. Rosa Parks reportedly brought quilts to one of these events.

1987

The MSU Museum publishes Michigan Quilts: 150 Years of a Textile Tradition.

1993

The Alliance for American Quilts forms to find ways to centralize information about quilts and their makers.

1999

Grant-funded research and development begins for the Quilt Index.

2003

The Quilt Index goes live as the first searchable online quilt database of its kind.

2018

The Quilt Index is upgraded. New site provides more visual appeal and information is architected "relationally," giving users better, more intuitive access to the index's vast stores of information.

Photograph by Doug Elbinger, courtesy of the Michigan State University Museum.

The David Quilt

BY **Marsha MacDowell** AND **Mary Worrall**

In 1985, the Michigan State University Museum launched the Michigan Quilt Project, which aimed to systematically document Michigan quilting history. At Quilt Discovery Days held around the state, community members brought in their quilts to be photographed and documented. At one of the early events, a couple brought in a quilt with a central star design. The owners knew little about the quilt except that it was thought to have been made by a Native American woman known as Anna or Margaret David. The David quilt was similar but different from other Star-pattern quilts: The corner squares as well as the triangular shapes along each side were appliquéd with boldly shaped, colorful flowers and leaves. The motifs clearly referenced the floral designs used by local Anishinaabek peoples, mostly those from Odawa and Ojibway tribes, in their beadwork.

Within a month, another Star quilt made of similar fabrics and with similar bold floral appliqué was brought to a Discovery Day. The quilt's owner recounted that her father had acquired the quilt in trade for some goods. An artist known to the family as Mrs. Ogamahgegado had made it; it was a cherished item, never used, and always simply referred to as "the Indian quilt." Subsequent research on Mrs. Ogamahgegado revealed that she lived in an Odawa settlement known as Ahgosa Town, in Michigan's Lower Peninsula.

David's quilt was selected as the cover of *Michigan Quilts: 150 Years of a Textile Tradition* (MacDowell and Fitzgerald, Eds., 1987), a book that reported on the initial findings of the Michigan Quilt Project. In the early 1990s, a member of the Little Traverse Bay Band (LTBB) of Odawa Indians alerted the MSU Museum about a quilt made by family member Susan Miller. When Frank Ettawageshick, a traditional potter and former LTBB chairperson, saw the *Michigan Quilts* book cover, he contacted the MSU Museum to say that he too owned a similar quilt, inherited from his father. The Shelburne Museum in Vermont also owns a quilt in this style, long attributed to a Plains Indian maker. Based on research done at the MSU Museum, however, this attribution has been changed to an anonymous Odawa artist from Michigan.

This particular combination of central star and appliquéd sections appears unique to the Anishinaabek living in the Traverse Bay region of Michigan. MSU Museum staff have continued to explore quiltmaking among Indigenous peoples in this region and have located more examples of similar quilts. In the 1930s, the *Detroit News* published an article about the newspaper's quilt show, a major annual event of the era, and included a photograph showing three judges holding up a quilt made by a Native American woman. "Bright colors predominate and the combination of flowers and patches is interesting," said the caption.

The discovery of the David quilt has led to many research, exhibition, and collection development activities focused on Native American quilting by the MSU Museum team. This includes a touring exhibition, *To Honor and Comfort: Native Quilting Traditions*, with the Smithsonian National Museum of the American Indian. The MSU Museum now holds what is considered the largest collection of Indigenous American quilts in the world. 𝒬𝑓

Quiltfolk is proud to collaborate with the American Quilt Study Group (AQSG) on this Trunk Show, an intimate look at one extraordinary quilt.
For more information on AQSG's mission, visit americanquiltstudygroup.org.

ON THE CUTTING TABLE

———

As we wrap up Issue 08, so many of the wonderful images
we captured did not make it into the featured stories.
Here are just a few of our favorites. Thank you to everyone who
shared their stories and spaces with us.

Bonus features from Michigan await you at *Quiltfolk.com*.
Because there's always more to the story.

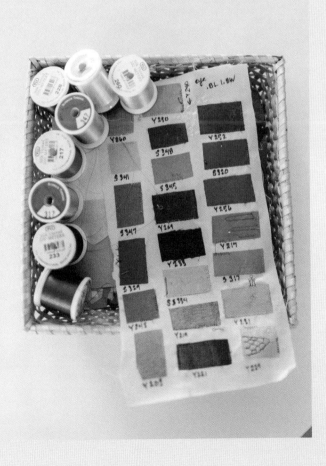